Thank you Sa

I hop

Andi

The beginning.

(All the credits and legal shit.)

Published By CYMprint

HEAVYWEIGHT THOUGHTS

(OF A LIGHTWEIGHT THINKER)

First Printing September 2021

Cover design – AJ Chamberlain
Cover Image by Daniel Kiener.

For more information contact the author:
www.AndiJamesChamberlain.com
www.facebook.com/wordsfromandi

ISBN - 978-0-9934016-4-0

ALSO BY ANDI JAMES CHAMBERLAIN.

One Man And His Dogma - A Novel

10 Short Of 31 - 31 Short Fictions and Confessionals

Heavyweight Thoughts
(of a lightweight thinker)

The Collected Poetry and Prose Of

ANDI JAMES CHAMBERLAIN

Introduction.

In 1998 - after a few lost years drifting wildly after quitting my A-Levels - I took the then life-changing decision to stop everything, quit my job, throw in for all I had and go back to college.

I was invited to see a friend perform in a play at Stratford Upon Avon College on one random Wednesday evening. Though I cannot remember what play it was, nor much from my life prior to attending, I do remember that it changed something in me fundamentally and set a spark inside my brain that would not subside until I applied for the same course myself and… I don't know…

Just.

Stop.

Drifting.

When I started college I would carry a small notepad and pen in my pocket everywhere I went and would write page after page of weird, disjointed, mostly terrible poems and small pieces of prose that was covered in odd doodles and strange scribbles. Inspired by everyone and everything around me.

When I eventually signed up for a further two years to continue my course into higher education, I met a brilliant fellow named James Edwards who became my closest friend and who I have - criminally - drifted further from in my advancing years since then, but who remains loved and inspirational to me to this day.

James carried a book and a pen as well.

I soon discovered he also was inspired by all the college offered and the people and the minutiae of everyday life… and his work was effortless.
His writing was beautifully succinct, funny as all hell and so raw and honest. Little stick men representations of all our classmates, tiny three-line poems about his life and how his day was going. Jarringly honest insights into a genuinely wonderful man's mind.

He inspired me then, he inspires me now.

There is little confusion why my first novel ONE MAN AND HIS DOGMA was dedicated to him.

I would sit up with him writing and drawing doodles, stickmen stories that were hysterical to us and had deeply hidden ciphers you could only decode if you were present in the room where the incidents happened. It was James who got me to take writing seriously.

Hours long conversations about art, music, respect for your influences and those who inspire - until every hour of the morning. Animated debates and gossips over full English's in the deli cafe.

Every word of it translated into stickmen drawings, and two or three-line poems, which I stole wholesale and added my own twist and started writing like my life depended on it.

That was James's influence that was.

All this is to say… the collection you have in your hands now is a direct result of those conversations. Those wistful hours spent dunking biscuits in cups of tea and talking about how many pictures of George Harrison he was surrounded by on the day Harrison died.

Hours making ridiculous interpretative dance moves that we would employ - like a ninja flash mob - in class and lecture, laughing stupidly at how hilarious we thought we were. The many, many times we drank fancy coffees whilst dissecting movies on the sofa or making stupid new theme songs to TV shows we all watched as a group like a ritual, every Monday evening.

This is a collection of writing and poetry that existed then and has been written in the intervening years since. Thoughts, musings, coded messages to certain someone's, poetries about love, life, death, war, peace, coffee, romance, hatred and every emotion and shade in between.

I do not profess to be a poet.

Truth be told, the reason this collection is so expansive - covering over 20 years of written work - is because I have never really been confident enough to put it all together and read it without judging myself harshly. I wrote all of this as it was running roughshod through my mind, and the stream of consciousness was easier to be ascribed to paper than left rampant around my mind.

I don't know if any of this is good or not - I have kind of always had a mental blocker on when it comes to poetry - that what I write is maybe not traditional, doesn't follow well established mechanics of poetical flow or thought. I may be butchering every established rule…

I don't know.

What I do know is that - beside James - one other person continually had my back throughout those twenty years. Someone else played cheerleader for my writing - especially my short form poetry and free thought prose. So much so that on more than one occasion he took my notebooks and would unveil them at social events and parties reading bits and pieces for everyone to listen too.

He would gleefully consume every word with a huge smile plastered all over his face and would critique (*always with exceptional positivity*) and would give me ideas and little suggestions, always pushing for me to exceed the previous piece of writing and improve and push my own limitations.

My dear old Dad. Melvyn Chamberlain.

My short story collection 10 SHORT OF 31 is dedicated to him. Throughout my entire life he has read my stories, he has actively sought out my work and pushed for me to share stories and ideas with him. We have had debates about everything you can imagine - from love, philosophy, politics, loss, ambition and everything in between.

He has never judged me; he has always called me on occasions I have rested on my laurels or fallen back on cliché and easy ideas. He has always been the driving force behind me continuing to TRY and be a writer. Without him, I would not have two books available - this book would be a wistful tendril of smoke on the ether - and I would probably be really, really miserable.

So Immeasurable thanks to both of these brilliant men.

The book you hold in your hands is written by me, inspired by twenty years plus of life, laughter, love, loss, learning, success and mistake - and was fuelled by the two wonderful inspirations who kept me on the course to just write, write, write.

I owe them a debt of massive gratitude.

I hope that I can clear my debt sometime in our lifetimes.

... Now.

This collection of writings you hold in your hand is yours.

You.

Dear reader.

I hope you enjoy what I have put together. I hope you find something that resonates, and I hope that you do not judge my amateur fumblings in poetry too harshly.

Know this, above all else, I *REALLY* enjoyed writing some of these pieces. Some manifested at the best times of my life, others at my lowest ebb. There is allegory, metaphor and hidden meanings buried in each and every piece. Occasionally poems are about specific people - names coded into titles - some of these names are lost even to me - buried under years of debris inside my brain.

Whoever you are, one or more of these may even be about you. So do not try and read too deeply into the imagery. I have never meant my words to harm, merely to heal my own chaotic mind.

Some of these pieces were written in a fit of passion in the moment, inspired by some ephemeral burst of inspiration I will never recall, but I hope that they resonate with you and you find solace, meaning and magic in the words.

Mostly, I hope that you find some enjoyment somewhere throughout.
I tried, and that - as my dear old dad keeps saying - is what really matters.

Maybe I will make some more of this. A Volume II, twenty years from now. A lifetime away yet just around the corner.

For now. Thank you.

Thank you for giving me a moment of your day.

Thank you for allowing a lightweight thinker to share these heavyweight thoughts with you.

Now.

On with the show.

Andi James Chamberlain

Leicester - July 2020.

DEDICATION:

Even though a special thanks is reserved for James Edwards and Melvyn Chamberlain I want to dedicate this book to the other voice of reason and inspiration that has constantly been both an influence and a thorn in my side.

My brother.

Thank you Gareth.

This ones for you.

Contents.

Shorts & Prose...

Poetry.

All the Presidents men.

And my God
It's getting pretty serious
someone needs to activate
his holiness the president
so he can just carpet bomb
third world countries
to maintain relevance
hoping people will forget
but we all remember
just like the elephants.

Radio rentals.

An untuned radio
is buzzing in my head.
Static rivers washing over
like a tsunami of noise
and a chattering of hyenas
screaming.
The door is open,
the window wide.
Yet here I am, still inside.

’Tis a lark.

Bull-whipped bones

creak and crunch as morning

is shaken from my

overtired frame.

Once to bed

now to rise again.

Lycanthropy.

The words that tumble

from mind and mouth

to open ear

and sewing circle.

Secrets warping into

rumour shifting in

some lycanthropy into

truth...

Inkwell.

Pure white quill dipped in jet-black ink
dripping life on ragged parchment.
A scrawl of words.
A mess of thought
and all of this straight from the soul.

When head and heart
both work as one
the words add up and the job gets done.

A writers life for me.

Stagger.

The taste of your name

is a ghost upon my tongue.

The bitterness is vibrant

the memory distant.

A confusion between the spheres.

Vicarious.

I wonder how many people I have watched die
on the TV screens and silver-screens and
tiny little mobile screens,

that we stuff in pockets and forget about;
until the monkey on your shoulder
comes tap, tap, tapping

and you can't help but answer
your mistress's call again.

I wonder how many people
I have watched die.
Over and over again.

Old movies rewatched a thousand times
the same man experiencing death
one hundred million styles.

A purgatory of story and sin.

The rivers all run in the same direction.

I am doomed to repeat the same mistakes.

Pushing people I love away,

because I cannot curb my pride

not even for a second

to keep my promise.

Stain.

I prefer to kill in analogue
I hate this lazy digital murder
precision weapons for wholesale slaughter
are no substitute for a blade on the throat.
I prefer my killing with a little bit of laughter.

My hands are rarely clean.

Light / Dark.

"Get in the taxi with me..."
You said.
even though we were separated by 40 Miles.
"Keep me company whilst I go head home,
stay with me, stay on the phone."
You laughed, a lot, I recall.
You said come over,
you'd pay for a taxi and all.
You told me secrets of what you had done, of things that had happened
places you'd gone.
And then you arrived at your own front door,
you said "hang up, I'll skype you
and we'll talk more!"

I remember smiling, more than I had for a while.
You made me laugh, and my heart beat faster.
You showed me your bedroom
shared your loves and your desires
you offered me Uber to carry me miles.
And then I slept, forty minutes on video,
woke to your friends like a smiling idiot.
And you still carried on, talking and laughing
and then said "tomorrow, I'll come and see you."

(And you did.)

The witches and the lamb.

Around the cold and musty Gyre
the coven met, warmed through by fire.
A damp and ugly mist was rolling
and though the hills were dark and swollen
with sounds of beast and burden weary;
The witches council came to meet.

"Fair welcome to thee, this black hued e'en."
Words spat through broken teeth
the air was thick with the stench of berry.
White milky eyes
and cackle merry;
The witches came for mass.

A whip-crack burst of hellish flame
popped from the cauldron, dark and eerie
the laughter thick, the air was drained
the light from moon above the council
dipped silently betwixt cloud quite bashful
the witches all hocked wads of phlegm
toward the fire, that burst again.

Here, amongst the Witches
we witness evil, hatred, pain.
Mottled skin, dried dead tongues,
hair that tangled and fell out in clumps.
Eyes half blind and hearts black as pitch.
The lonely existence of the witch.

The clouds above parted gently,
the mist was thick but crept in silence,
the moon shone down, bright and hearty,
the valley lit up like a lighthouse beacon
and the animals paused quick and fearful.
Noses raised toward the sky...

Something, somewhere, was about to die.

"A sacrifice! That's why we gather!"
The lead witch said through torn lipped slather
"A knife drawn sharply cross the throat!"
The council all replied in croak.
"Blood and gristle! Bone and meat,
cut the throat and let us feast!"
And the lead ghoul raised a hand quite neatly,
one finger raised and pointed weakly,
upon the crowd, here bayed and gathered...

"You!" She screamed
stabbing finger - more bone than flesh,
upon a witch now drenched moist in gloom.
"You shall be our goat this e'en,
we'll cut your throat and dissect your spleen.
We'll rip apart your heart and liver...
Yes! You..."
She laughed and drooled...
"You shall be our gift to the moon"

They lay her down on a slab of granite;
tied her hands with the guts of rabbit.

Gagged her mouth with cruel dirty rags
and pulled her taut
as hard as they can.
The knife was raised and glinted merrily
"Farewell sister, you feed the earth,
your fate was set from the moment of birth.
Your blood and bone will feed us well
you'll save us all, whilst you rest in hell"

The sacrificial lamb to slaughter,
this wanton slattern, this demon's daughter,
begged with her eyes for the gag to be slackened,
the council complied as well as able,
and the lamb said gently through cracked black lips...

"Thank you, sisters, live ye long,
steal babes from cots
and creatures from stables ,
and when the time comes that ye join,
you'll find seats saved at the devils table"

Mutha.

Take action!
Take some motherfucking pride in reaction.
Retraction, on the other side of detracted comments

CENSOR YOURSELF!
CENSOR YOUR DREAMS!

Find a motherfucking message to scream.
Nothing as it seems,
living the consequence, a subject of means.

FRONTAL ASSAULT!

Take up a stance, head the revolt.
Pushed back to forever
we need to halt.

COMPASSION!

Get a motherfucking dose of passion!
Blast out the songs that unite us to them,
bring up the banners,
press play to begin.

Stop hiding behind surprise
stop hiding and realise;
We are the future.
We are the seed.
We can't be stopped.

You have to see to believe.

We are the journey.
We are the key.
Payment of nothing,
actively free,
Numbered so many you can't hold us back.
Push us too hard we are poised to attack.

Motherfucking land of the free?
Motherfucking land for the lost?
Motherfucking maniac in charge -
is all out to lunch.

Push it out, we pull it in.
See us fall? We dive in and swim.

Retraction of statements,
motion to repeal.
Hold on for glory
we need to reveal.

Take up the charge-
we head to the sky.
Smoking our doctrine,
are we stoned? are you high?

Are we real?
You're so false?
Are we needed?
Do *you* see *us*??

Nothing but a motherfucking circus of rust.

We see you.
We hear you.
We know you,
and it's you we don't trust.

Motherfucker.

Autumn / omy.

Take the names,
play the games
but never be a footstool for the man.

Kick the leaves
and throw them dice
but never be a figure for the stats.

Kiss the girls
and fuck the police
but never be a cog in the systems wheels.

Playing possum
mixing lessons
but never tell the secret you have learned.

I am the circle
you are the square
always infallibly human

But never fucking there.

Chandleresque.

Old broken records
always play faster
on the scratches.

The tune will never play
when needle catches rivet.

Mixed up again
replaying the same note forever.

An eternity of the same rhythm
'til the death of vinyl.

Catch 23.

We can drop the bomb
but will we really stop the war?
Some would say
religion is the way.

I say its quarter to deadline and God still isn't here.

So give her a call
let's hope that she appears.
'Cos we are running on empty
and your call still isn't in…

and those Riders are taking the streets.

Waving the flag won't stop them.
Just give up your future
pledge your faith to the past.

O'death is upon us
and this time it will last.
It's time to meet your maker
to lay your cards upon the deck

So, smile and think
of violence and war.
Present me your neck
please close your jaw.

Wave goodbye to anger
say goodbye to pain.
We'll cut the umbilical to the last world
and film the birth of the new.

Please sign on this line here,
and we'll begin again.

(Yossarian lives.)

Contemplation cocktail.

Make the silence last a little longer
potency of these feelings
becomes a little stronger.

Love is an hourglass.
Madness, one grain at a time.
The state I attained without you.

Becoming the catalyst in this war.
The brick in the pavement that breaks my back.
The fist that slacks my jaw.

Hello me.

Cheese.
So they call me, so I am.
Cheesus.

The Mozzarella Messiah
The Gorgonzola God
The Red Leicester Lord

Holy Trinity of Dairy.
Cheesus.

So I will be.
Turning water into Philadelphia,
and instead of curing the blind man
I instead give him a mini Babybel
and hope he gets well soon.

After all, being a saviour is a hungry job.
Stilton, anyone?

Japanese paper.

Freezing, feeling
from lip to fingertip.
I must warm this heart of mine.

All I need is a little more time,
all I ask is for a little more time.
Bleeding, streaming
from nerve to sacred breath.

I must accept that age is so unkind.
Breathing,
needed more than needing,
dead.

Breathing more than living,
Led.

Delicate like the petals
falling from a cherry blossom,
landing on the paper
that melts under your touch.

Red sun setting.
Waves a-shore are lapping.
Day above now down below,
the stars begin to shimmer on the sea.

Sepia and slate.

Dead leaves crushed to powder
under winter heel,

frostbitten and dancing
on crisp grassy carpet.

Blunted sun hiding
behind misted, muted sky.

The world is clotted
in sepia and slate.

The laughter shrouded
amongst sniffles and
sneezes. spring awaits.
Small buds of optimism
poking through.

Life, that beautiful spectrum,
of colour and joy,
ready for another round.

Rumpelstiltskin.

If you're waiting
for the ponytail, to drop
out of a window,
from a tower that is several storeys high,
which was discovered because
a voice was floating
melodically on the breeze,
and you followed hoping
Princesses we're looking
for a Prince.
Or you killed a dragon,
and have slain a witch,
to see the sleeping girl
that is rumoured to exist
in the castle hidden deep
within the thicket.
You need to remember
not all princesses
need a prince,
not all sleeping beauties
need a kiss to revive and

warm their spirits.
Not all towers are prisons,
and the world is not a fairy tale
that you can manipulate to
your advantage.
To be better than you are.
There is a need for authenticity
not make-believe and fantasy.
So be yourself,
and do what's right,
and avoid the forests
and things that bump in the night.
Be a real man, not a model of one.
A gentleman, a scholar,
a student and learner,
always look to better
that which came before.

Not a knave who looks for danger,
when you could just knock upon the door.

The Bowman.

Every errant arrow
from the quiver to the sparrow
is tinged with devout sadness
as the 'head pierces the heart.

Lick spittle fires snap
hot coke falls from grille
to wrap roughshod upon
the carpet tinder,
Inferno finds no guard to hinder.

Lazy laps of fierce charnel heat
spreads like honey from wall to seat.
Weak timber creaks
greased pangs of agony
as the beams above evolve to ash.

Smoke tendrils wind around young lungs
flesh and sinew mingle,
muscles groan, thoughts waft and flutter,
as tired eyes collapse
and tiny hearts A-Tingle.
Excitedly we burn,
our breathing now a labour,
our cries for help a muted stutter.

Planetary Express.

A slither of a silver lining
a minute in minutiae
breaking down the atoms
into fractions, reactions
a stumbled attraction
like a magnet lay in mercury.
A deaf foreman of the jury,
unaware of consequence
and ignorant of bliss.
A punch in the mouth
when you expected a kiss
shock and awe, we give you peace
you crave violence more.

Alexander Graham Bell.

We are all connected

but all our lines,

they seem engaged.

DEATH: (*To the audience*).

Where once I rode
with but three companions
and though we reaped and wrought our Tithe and Tally
with fervour and thirst

(though always with a solemn sense of duty and eternally unbiased execution)

Now!
Now, my stable swells to bursting
with stallion and mare,
my cup runneth over
with young, voracious riders of the storm.
Vigorous, hungry-to-impress squires,
clutching at the reins
white knuckled,
red throated
and ready
to be called forth to meet
upon yonder reaping fields.

Smoke monster.

This isn't fear
this is madness
wading through layers and layers
of sadness.
I'm so lost in this bleak shrouded darkness
striving and clinging and reaching for light.

Reaching for light.

This party is a riot.

Don't drown in an entitlement wave
waiting in vain
for the crowd to chant
your name.
Bleating and tweeting
hideous doctrine
the masses begin to
decode your chagrin.

Your lies will soon come out
the people now know
what you are all about
the kool-aid effect is starting to fade.

Debutante.

The first crisp autumn frost has fallen.
Under foot it crunches
in satisfying tones of brittle bladed beauty.

Winter is encroaching from the shadows
the seasons are retreating
toward the dawn of the new year.

The cold snap heralds scarves and gloves
snow is looming from above
and soon we will be hanging out that mistletoe.

The days are falling off the calendar
and we know that candles ebb out slowly.
The crisp autumn frost whispers from underneath your clumsy foot.

The land is white, and fog is shrouded
greens are muted and skies are clouded
and the autumn settles into bones and blades of grass and windowpanes.

The year begins its tumble to the end.

Beyond echoes.

Intermittent
this transmission
echoes, beyond all recognition.
These preached words
mostly repetition,
just repeat these superstitions.

Echoes, beyond our understanding
lost between the fall and landing,
trapped in static,
our morals stranded,
we pay our dues,
with cash we're handed.

Echoes, beyond the veil
of dreaming.
faces in the white noise screaming,
we stand our ground with passions piqued,
blood is rushing,
heartbeats unique.

Our love a sword to pierce the future
we assert our art
we support our culture,

we circle our craft
like hungry vultures.

Community - an army marching,
our talents glow
warm, demanding.

Spreading wings to fly away
when music plays, we stand and sway
because beyond that which echoes
and that which shakes
love will blossom
and fear, it will break.

In those cracks of darkness, light.

When our heroes fall to evil,
conquered by the might.
Where passion falters,
the brave surrender
cornered by some blight.
When hopes warm glow is dulled,
left rusty, and two wrongs
do not make a right.
Where shadows shroud
and slither silent,
and the skies gold shines less bright,
remember this, and rise united.
With voice as raspy as a razor,
and heart fit sharp to boom.
The sun may set in cold abandon,
it's warmth and love will soon
meander, from the east to stretch
and tendril,
finding nooks and crannies tight,
filling every space and volume
once black and angered,
now so full and fit to bursting -
look close, look close, ye curious sparrow -
and yonder now the sight.
Where once was black and misbegotten -
transformed, renewed and now quiet.
The haze removed, the veil upended
and in those cracks of darkness, light.
Only light.

The Prince (II).

Machinations that are machiavellian.
One step ahead of you
like a Marvel villain.
Slick, sharp and dastardly,
why won't this bastard see?
Carnival barking
that they're so far advanced from me.

Slip shod, ruined and odd,
struggling for leverage
when here, still, i'm stood.
Can't see the forest for all of these woods,
constantly damning all the
woulds, coulds and shoulds.

Romantic rapscallion, a mischievous muse.
Just don't light a spark,
because I have a short fuse.
Prone to explosions, an unfortunate symptom…
take these pills to calm nerves,
creating a simpleton.

Carving a niche with a hammer and axe,
you need to be patient,
not just wantonly hack.
Shapes don't come fluid
it's a matter of luck.
But sooner or later your creation is free.
a tiny reminder - that once was a tree

45.

Fumes, winding tendril.
Runes, raising tensions.
Wrapped around my organs
and threatening to squeeze.

The world breathes out
as the worst president leaves.
A culmination of incompetence,
ashes smoulder in open fire.

A final goodbye to an accomplished liar.

Prevaricate.

All these lies
we try to tell ourselves
to help improve our lives
often go the other way.
Have you ever held a lie?
slipping out your hands,
impossible to grasp,
a shadow that tries to
dodge your touch.
Leaves you stood like an idiot.
They all collect in the night,
gathering inward
turning dignity to dust
and breaking every trust.
We try,
to pull on every thread,
to put the pieces back to one,
but fragments always find a way…
to disappear in the dark.

- How am I meant to -

build it all back up again?
To repair the hopes and fears,
to make it like it used to be.
Have you ever held a lie?
It's cold and it eats you;
it makes it hard to feel alive

Not that you ever were.

Apres la deluge.

A crack in the riverbed
can create a brand new river.
Diversion of the waters
slowly seep, flow and slither.
A monument to disaster
a deluge of coincidence;
crashing through your neighbourhood
and creating change much faster
than the universe can muster.
Changing landscapes
shifting perception.
A natural remedy too gentrification.
Waters ebb and flow
cascading and rolling,
this flood is mechanical;
unstoppable, untenable.
devastation now a side-effect
of natures awesome spectacle.
Before me the flood.
Behind me the river.
Once humanity would take, take, take…
but now we are forgivers.
Dancing in the water, with
a new sense of gratitude.
Our dulled emotions fixed,
now a full change in attitude.
A crack in the riverbed -
signed, sealed and delivered.

Ghosts of old ideas.

All these sexual politics
are getting, frankly, complicated;
yet here I am again
sexually frustrated.
I watch the ghosts of old ideas
get deeply desecrated
I wish I could say something
but instead, again, I hesitated.

So I hold my breath
count to ten
think of something good to say,
something fast and witty
that will help me save the day,
but instead my brain
revolts again
and I am left here pondering.

No words, no lies, no repartee
to help me round her in,
instead, back to the beginning
I collapse as we start again.
There is no saving grace
as I fall flat, teeth chattering

The world begins to spin
I cannot stop it happening;
so I face the final days
with panicked heart and stupid grin.

Siren song.

Restless waters
run deep.
At least that's what they say.

A Siren song
calling me to the rocks,
but don't worry, my love

I was headed there anyway.

Sorry, pardon me.

Nice and vague.
Vaguely bobbing, like an apple
on an ocean, in the grip
of a current that you cannot sway.

Enter the fray,
have your say.
Find solutions to the problems,
there will always be a way.

Positive you're negative?
Negate the need to be,
complacent or evasive
or all that's in-between.

The way to secure victory
is by coming out the winner.
Enjoy what's on your plate,
chow down that chicken dinner.

Remember to say thank you
Sorry, pardon me.
There's ways to not
be a sinner.

You'll see.
Believe me.

Magna Carta.

Conform.
Make a mission, in remission of a subject
once quite mooted as taboo.
Boo-Fucking-Hoo.
Cooking my shoes to make stew
that's enough for me, but what about you?
Introverted retrospective.
Sending out a signal for a new civilisation.
This is some funky shit.
Mixing it up with the writers of the hits,
got the shits, like a verbal diarrhoea,
onomatopoeia - mixing up my meanings…
Metaphorical like a magnet,
alliterate this
riddle me that
fixing a hole in my coffin
so I keep nice and dry.
We all die.
Like a sonic innuendo,
voices climaxing to crescendo
You try to make a million
instead end up with a pit.
Sick of this shit,
coins in a fountain are all I have to keep
me from running to the border
a new world order, board painted black

and bored bored bored of all this crap.
Burn bright, Saturday night,
stomping down dark alleyways,
looking for a fight.
Bite - like a dog or a cougar,
shoot fast, German Luger,
using my broom to beat back what you want.
Haunted like a mansion full of ghosts
of memories and melody.
A lamentation of the way we live our lives today,
and not of who we were.
May I take you to the dance?
So that we may prance,
and act devoid of all abandon
and relate to all these tokens that
we never once did own.
Snatching glory from defeat,
and binging on the meat,
this is what it is
to try and keep afloat.
My mind is a Titanic,
Iceberg pierced and
slowly sinking.
Confused, distracted and
barely making sense.
No longer am I divine -
These lords are signing away my majesty.
Magna Carta.

Drowning on fresh air and circumstance.

Follow your eyes
let the sunshine blind you.
Drown in the gold
let the universe surround you.
Breathe in this mystery,
this symmetry,
the asinine delivery.
breathe in and think of me…
aching and falling
please stop all the stalling,
all of these reasons and lies
are not a surprise
i've come to expect it of you.
Believe in seasons,
forget the obvious reasons,
the fears of the past
count to ten and fall at last
and let your life flash past your eyes
one image at a time,
until you are left with nought but dimes
and slowly understand
that this is how it's meant to be.

Breathe in, and think of me.

Another obstacle of youth.

Sometimes I feel
like I am all alone
no obvious reason
to be like I am.
Other times I want to contemplate
why you would leave me?
Is it me you hate?

I have no motive
I am meaningless
with the feeling - you don't now
nor ever cared less.
And when I see you
I feel a vacuum in my heart.
Everything within
is slowly taken from me…

I want to watch the sun
to see it's golden face again.
Watching solemnly
as a better race begins.
And though it won't be long
I doubt I will be there at the end,
because even though I love you
it feels better this way my friend.

My thoughts are an island now
surrounded by roaring floods,
and healing won't do anything
to set me free,
because all I see
is you.

Another bitter sign of truth.
One more counter to my act.
Another obstacle of youth.

Director Denial.

There's not a secret
I cannot figure
out a solution
using a system.

Breaking the codes of
conduct and passion.
Leaving a trail of
breadcrumbs to follow.

Come one come all.
Come one come all.

Help me to help myself
tempt not the tempter tempting you.
Help me to help myself.
I am over you.

Time is a healer
like any other
shall I be mother?
All these babies to smother.
We are illusions,
failing to read you.
Tell me your secret.
I will believe you.

Help me to help myself.
Because I am over you.

This is a new start.
Lambs to my slaughter,
try not to hear me,
ignore my laughter.
I am an angel
you are a demon.
Stamp out my rivals,
with a seal of approval.

Help me to help myself.
I am so over you.
I am so over you.
I am so over you.

This is what happens when we give robots knives.

Everything appears so blue
and it all connects to you.
I don't want to hear your lies
it comes to me, as no surprise
that every lie I said to you
is true.

I am waiting / I am hiding
I am you.

Everything you say is true
comes back to haunt you.
I am so sick of winning second prize
I see stories in your eyes.
Such a surprise.
Such a surprise.
Such. A. Surprise.

I am waiting / I am hiding
I am you.

Look under your bed tonight
and tell me what you see.
Look into my eyes tonight,
and tell me what you see.

Look on top of the mountain tonight
and tell me what you see.
Look under your bed,
and tell me what you see.
Tell me what do you see?

Tell me what do you see?

I am waiting,
I am hiding.
I am you.

Dentistry for beginners.

You are so soft to touch
tender skin - to be part of this sin,
make me feel so alive.
I - want to be inside you
I - want to be part of you
I - want to carry you all away.

Breathe me deeper.
Let me soak you skin,
kissing the one you love
with a mouthful of broken teeth.

I - want to be part of you.
I - want to carry you.
I want to carry you away.

There is sin upon your skin
cool to touch
but not too much,
don't get carried away.

I - want to be inside you.
I - want to be part of you.
I don't want to get carried away.

Breathe me deeper.

Let me soak your skin.
Kissing the one you love
with a mouthful of broken teeth.

Love me.
Carry me.
Cherish me.
Bury me.
Trust me.
Hold me.
Love me, love me, love me.

Won't - you pity what I am?
Silently,
I turn away
I am lost again,
and I cannot find my way.

I - want to be inside you.
I - want to be part of you.
I want to carry you.

Don't get carried away.

Pity me,
Cherish me,
Love me,
Fuck me,
Fucking carry me.

Love me - love me - love me.

I want to carry you,
carry you far away.

With my blood, we can see through the sun.

Is this what makes you happy?
Killing me one day at a time?
Is this what makes you happy?
Treating love like it's a crime?

And with my blood
we can see through the sun.
And with this blood,
we can stare straight at the sun.

Today is a good day to die.

I am sacrificed,
I am hung out to dry.
Today is a good day to die.

I hope this is what makes you happy.

Odyssey.

Take my burden on you.
So that I may sleep.
It's all I want too…

Won't you let me sleep?

It's all I want too…
Won't you let me sleep?

Pandora.

Listen to the sound of clockwork priests.
Fire purifies the ruined streets.
Unwanted tears from tired eyes.
All of this love begins to die.

And all these feelings boxed up as a child -
are returned and free.
The Pandora wild.

Things will never be the same.

And so the circle,
begins anew.
We hold on, us precious few.
And so the circle,
begins anew
and we hold on, us precious few…

Now that Pandora is wild.

Sado-monarchism.

I would…
kill the Gods above for you.
And I would…
bury kings and queens alive for you.
And I would…
cleanse everyone we love for you.
And I would…
burn everything I have for you.

But only you.
Yes, only you.

I would…
kill all the Gods above for you.
And I would…
bury kings and queens alive for you.
I do all of this…
But only for you.

Check your facts.

Feed me your lies
let me devour.
Murdered in print
my reputations in tatters.
These are my secrets, these are my lies

Please let me help you,
Please let me try.

Please let me have one day.
Please God, one day before I die.
Please God won't you say I tried?
Please God - won't you make it so?

Check your facts.
Before they kill you.

All hail the Elephant-man.

Feed the lions
to the Christians.
Take the light out of my fathers eyes.
Shut your mouth and listen.
It's time for your faith to fly.
Come on.

Shut your mouth and listen
because your better is about to speak.
Shut your mouth and listen,
to these words I preach.

Because everywhere you run
and everywhere you fall
and everywhere you hide,
you are always facing destiny,
come on.

You're God will forgive you
but I cannot let that be.
Your God will forgive you,
But I simply cannot let that be.
Bring vengeance to me.
Bring vengeance.
I will see you cursed.

Smile, victory is in the air.
Smile, victory has come tonight.

Everywhere you stand,
and everywhere you fall,
you're always facing destiny.
And though your God will forgive you,
I cannot let that be.
Bring vengeance to me.
Bring vengeance to me.
I will see you hang.

I am the Elephant-Man
I am the Elephant-Man.
I am the Elephant-Man.

All hail the Elephant-Man

Tiger in a hurricane.

Never going to see me again.
First i'm a shape
then i'm a shadow,
like a Tiger in a hurricane.

Never going to see me again.
Never going to see me again.
Never going to see me again.

Tiger in a hurricane.
Tiger, Tiger -
burning bright.
But where's the Tiger? Where has that Tiger gone?

Little children,
Why are you crying?
Little children,
Your parent have lied to you.
Tiger - is inside.

First a shape,
then a shadow.
But always inside.

Never going to see me again.
Never going to see me again.
Never going to see me again.

Death (and the high cost of living).

The sun will not rise tomorrow
its light has abandoned the sky.
The moon and the stars in sorrow,
have both laid down and died.
You and I
we will survive
until
we both die.

That is the light and the lie.

The moon and the stars together
both have abandoned the sky
the sun, ever so clever, has laid down and died.
You and I
we will survive
until
we too, die.

That is the light and the lie.

We, all get one chance.
One hope
One chance at life.
So why are we ruining it -
with lies, hate, brutality and…

I'm drained.

Whatever happened to honesty, love and respect?

You and I will survive
even as the sun lays down to die.
We will go,
high, high, high.

Because that is the light and the lie.

Look…
into the eyes of the people who you love.
Look…
Into the heart of the people who you trust.
There.
You'll find heaven there.
That is where you'll find God.
Look…
Into the heart of the people who you trust.
There.
You'll find heaven there, that's where you'll find God.

That's where you'll find God.

Burial ground.

Apathy is an empty gun
pointed at the cross.
And apathy is an empty cross
pointed at the sky.

It's hard to have a conversation with God
when all he does is walk away.
And all these Gods get down from their crosses
and walk away, they walk away.

We are the broken.
we are the damned.
We are the vultures - coming for your crown.

We are here,
We want the crown.

Kill your Gods
and start again.
Kill your Gods
and start again.

Because apathy is an empty gun
pointed at yourself.
Apathy is an empty cross,
hanging from your neck.

You say arson, I say viking funeral.

You will not find what you came here for.
You will not leave with what you came here for.
Carry me
Carry me away with my dignity.
Bury me
Bury me alive in tides of fire.

You will not find what you came here for.
You will not leave with what you wanted here.
Carry me.
Carry me away with me dignity
Bury me.
Bury me alive in tides of fire.

And when they say arson,
We say viking funeral.

Ten Tonne Mekon.

Deep, down, warm in my soul
I made a promise to carry you all.
A burden so sharp,
so heavy, so clean.
I bear it alone,
Deep, down, warm - inside my soul.

Bones are so brittle,
the sound is so harsh,
I pray that you make it,
as I stagger alone.

Deep,
Down,
Dark.
Inside my hole.

Please get me an angel I can call my own.

Deep,
Down,
Dark,
inside my soul.

If we make tomorrow,
I'll wake you, so you know.

Behind green eyes.

Insides are killing me
nothing else seems to be.
My future's soluble,
this bubbles burst
i'm gone.

I hold on, in spite of me
i'll be fine,
let me go.
Open eyes carefully,
it's time to start the show.

Every time I look at you
All I see are lies
hidden behind
your beautiful, beautiful…

Sheltered, i'm shelving these
faces, force-feeding me.
Flicker candle, rambling
burning all these pointless things.

And I shake these foundations down
I shout the founders down.
I shake foundations down
I shout the founders down.
And 1000 epileptics all nod to agree.

The patriots act.

Fumes wind round these ruins.
Memories and rumination
driftwood of some forgotten nation
a fragment of devastation
a totem to remember.

The false flags shiver
in the whispered gusts of the coming storm,
the slow crawl of a revolution
is conveniently borne.

The raised high fists
and stomped cobbled stones,
streets alive with rumbled grief,
the throng push on to hold their brief.

The Capitol is torn and shredded,
blood and sweat and terror dreaded
the red and blue and white power
the land of the brave scatters and cowers.

A single shot, an invader fallen
flagpoles broken
and windows caved in.
The republic cries tonight.

There are no truths
when the Big Lie rules.
Gold and orange is
the new red, white and blue.

Prmthn.

I stole the fire, to light up the pitch dark sky
and the promenade of Gods *(those hypocrites)*
punished me,
with chains, and rock,
leaving me in isolation
for crows to peck
my liver out. *(why can I not die?)*
This my penitence for taking that
which was always ours.

Every morning, the flesh consumed by birds.
Bloodied and beaten
as much as cattle fallen from the herd.
I wish my punishment
was that I were allowed to die -
instead - here I am in a hell of forever,
when there is no more liver,
my eyes become feast for the flock.

I took back this fire
was accused of theft,
but how can you steal that which was given freely -
and held in ransom by these bastard Gods.
(those heathens, those hellions)

I take this fire back - *Burn it all to ash*
As tribute to your faith - *Though I do not believe*
The world begins to Burn - *Please, allow me to watch*
Cleanse the Heavens, start again - *Reset, restart, rebirth.*

No longer will I be fodder for this murder of crows.

We need to talk about mother.

I remember only flickers.
Flashes.
Spots of time, long past and drifting on the jet-stream of memory.

She slept a lot.
Always sleeping.

In between bits.
The luminal spaces have shy glimpses of the good times;
when she would laugh. When she would play.

She wasn't good at jokes.
She was whip-sharp with witty retorts, rapier slashes that cut your own zinger down with a single swipe.

Charming too.
All to seldom are those memories though. Hidden
like vampires from the sunlight. Like the gremlins
amidst the circuitry of the machine.

But she was charming.

A shy smile, a cracked laugh and the fingers pushing
obsidian black lock over her ample ear.
The fingers slight and long.

"Witches fingers!"

She would say as she tickled my tummy, eliciting screeched giggles and guffaws.

But mostly, she slept a lot.

Morning, noon and night.
Curled up under blankets on the sofa,
disappearing to her bedroom and showing
no sign of life except those ugly cries to us both in the lounge,
eating crisp sandwiches
in front of some cartoon or another.

Hawkish moans and screams.
Words, unintelligible, spat and hollered down the stairwell,
the deranged mutterings of a sick woman.

She slept an awful lot.

Dinner was never missed. We were not neglected or forgotten,
abused or misbegotten.
We wanted for nothing. We were educated, clean and
well raised children...
but...
I can't remember the times when she cooked.

I can't recall a single dinner that she prepared or served me.
Not a Christmas lunch nor a birthday feast.
Not one.

I cooked.
My dad cooked. My brother attempted cheese on toast once or twice...
to varying degrees of failure.

But she did not cook.
Not that I can recall.
Not one meal since the night of the kitchen, and the knife.

Nine-to-five.

There is a storm within.
Brain and guts rumble like a thunderous
sheet of grey and gloom.
A sonic boom.
A driven front of frustrated
boredom, come to devastate
the calm island of my heart.

Ambition is a faulty starter motor
in an ageing car, smoking
broken, stalled at the side
of the busiest road.
The driver, stood lonely in the rain.

There has to be something,
anything, more than this.

Magpie mathematics.

Two magpies dancing,
a dandy little dalliance.
Shaking a tail feather
at the side of the road.
No sorrow for me today,
just joy. The birds will it so.
Onward we go.
My journey forward
shrouded in a wall of mist.
Rolling, crawling, creeping
heavy across the field and hill.
Behind me, my rearview mirror
shows blue skies and sunshine.
A metaphor?
Perhaps.
Maybe it's a cosmic joke.
Meaning, enshrined in paranoia.
Overcomplicating, overanalysing;
just… pay attention to the road.
Let's get to where you need to be.
Think of the magpies, dancing.
Two for joy.
Two for joy.
Two for joy.
Even if they were stood a few feet apart.
They were definitely friends
not just strangers,
birds of a feather,
dancing on the verge.

Two for joy.
I promise.

Human buffet.

Live my life
with constant inaction
a continuous series
of preprogrammed reactions

Living?
Or just breathing for something to do.
Gasping down a gulp or two.

Oxygen, mingling with my fire
backdraft causing a combustion.
Explosive and poignant,
revel in this self destruction.

Dying?
Just closing my eyes for something to do.
Snatching some peace for a moment or two.

Smoke under the doorframe,
conscious only of the pain.
The fizz and snap of fire licks
flesh becomes a canvas of blisters.

Burning?
Or just turning to ash,
as a tribute to you?
Well, either way, it's something to do.

Making promises
you know you will blunder.
Anger internal,
rumbling like distant thunder.

The rolling of storms,
bringing gusts, bringing gale.

Stand in the open expect rain,
get hale.

Loathing?
I turn on myself,
by turning these screws.
Punishing myself,
as penance to you.

After all,
I did say I wanted
a hobby or two.

What better than this?
It's something to do.

My scars.

It's fine that you stabbed me. I saw the blade months before I felt the cut,
before I felt the dark awful penetration of the blade in my back.
It's fine.
I would have preferred if you had straight up stabbed me in the heart,
but that's ok, in times like these we can't always get what we want.
Indeed, we would be lucky if we get to see the flash of silver before the knife
is twisted deeper in.
I have scars. So many of them.
Trophies they are of a time when my lapse in concentration, judgement
and sensibility has marked me with a memento-mori of a slither of life.
A memoriam of stupidity or love or madness,
a fleeting remembrance of a single second of void thought.
I have scars.
Fissures of skin, darkened or lightened on my body
to stand out as a badge of honour to show those moments
when we learn hardest. Pock marks and lines
of dead tissue line the back of my hands from brambles and thorns I climbed,
from the fences of my childhood
and hedges I bounded over; gates of rust and adventure from my lost youth,
in search of "*I don't know what*" but, searching
because it felt like the right thing to do.
It's fine that you stabbed me.
My body is a map of deep semi-healed wounds, lines of dead matter
that tell a thousand stories too long and crazy to tell to strangers,
like that time I…
ah! But I digress.
It's fine that you stabbed me… I expected it,
and all the while I knew it was coming, I saw the look in your eye
as you were waiting for me to unsheathe my blade first.

Waiting for me to force it into your flesh,
piercing your heart as you gasp out your contrived last breath...
"I always knew you'd do this" you would whisper as you evaporated into dust.
But I never did.
I never attacked.
I don't even own a knife.
Instead, I sat here, scars on show
– for the whole world to see –
adorning every inch of my being, illustrating a colourful history
of past indiscretions and mistakes,
and I smiled, because there was nothing else for me to do,
as you were stabbing my back again.
I wish it was my heart.
At least then I could have seen your eyes
judged for myself as you lunged the knife in to the hilt…
Was this murder?
Or was this self defence?

Thunderstorms in May.

This hollow…
this hollow frequency.
Fleeting between the stations,
sound collapsing in
like black-holes
drawing matter into the void
obliterating substance
and leaving dust.
Much like the shards of our love.
words are now so shallow
our voices raised
and anger like a static
filling the edges of the ether,
decayed transmissions
that slip roughshod
as hearts and minds
are overridden,
by noisy throats.
This crumbling love.
This fragmented desire.
The death of a star,
like the fall of the empire,
like the end of this great affair.
An era of amore
consequentially for nought.

For the price of a first class stamp.

Life changing?
I call it an embarrassment, you liar.
Shake my hand?
I'd rather cut your wrists, make you sing
nursery rhymes -
find some roses to ring.
Swinging songs for my baby.
It's hazy.
Have to admit, I feel a little lazy,
boy.
Lying on the tracks, what a dreamer -
On the inside, under skin,
I'm a faithless believer.
Truth will deny you something
and more than likely
you will deny yourself.
Swinging songs for my lady.
Virtually making love
through Royal Mail.
Intention, contended - rage against
this missed incentive.
Misconceived - embarrassed
by my apparent innocence.
My inner sense is telling me,
it yells at me
questions unanswered that
wink at me, strangely blinking

sinking -
like ships and cruisers,
these horrendous abusers,
frightful bruisers.
Floating around ambiguous
like a life-raft on a sea of doubt.

Shadowed.

Farewell, goodbye…
we all head off too tomorrow
I refuse to wear this hood
of guilt and sorrow
Farewell, goodbye…
this hole is now your hollow,
a grave that's far to shallow
lay down your head and go to sleep.

Because no matter what we do
this sin you carry
keeps on staining you.

Farewell, goodbye…
angel of honour
force-fed all these haunting
visions of tomorrow.
And tears will streak my cheeks
and we carry on down this road;
lost but unafraid,
led but never followed.

Faster vermin, faster.

Fields of dreams,
these errant voices chatter.
Changing of the ways,
these politics really matter.
My look of pure surprise
is really not surprising
when you consider the times
and the tone that you were using.

Over and over again,
my goodwill
you are abusing,
self-loathing and spreading lies
this life of your own choosing.

Lady Death embraces,
and the curtain's drawn on the end of days.
This pure rain pours hard down on me
and permeates my skin,
wash away confusion
highlight all these sins.

There is never any substance,
complete lack of something new.
These lies you keep on spreading,
look so very good on you.

As my weak heart waits to severe
all these bonds tied to the truth
whispers - wrapped in rumours
now so long in the tooth.

Trying to find my station -
my purpose in this life -
I'm an abject disaster,
daily trips on the hamster-wheel
with the whole world screaming
FASTER
VERMIN,
FASTER.

Untitled (I).

Cold pages
are thirsty
for delicious
fresh ink
gluttony unbuckled
guzzling sentences
peppered with
nouns and
adjectives, galore!

Carnivorous, this
poem. Devouring
thoughts and
feelings. Colour
and shade.
All light
and all
shadow, shrouded
in flavour
and bitter
forever after.
Cinnamon, spice,
candied rice.
A cornucopia of
cold pages

Open heart surgery.

A blade of dazzling light
bouncing from an abandoned
skylight, disrupting my uneasy
sleep, and dragging me back
to wakefulness again.
All thoughts and memories
of this evenings dreams
turn to whips of ash.
Inside my cloudy mind.
the brightness cuts, quite surgical
sharp and defined, steady
hands on radiant knives.
Peel away these layers
of dozy, vague ambivalence.
Drops of ice-cold perspiration
a herald to sudden violence.

Son of a preacher man.

Let me hit this bong
and my rhymes get high viscosity
doesn't do a thing
to slow down the velocity.
Come in hard and fast
like an arrow,
like an Exocet.
Struggling to handle this
think we'll have to call an exorcist.
Cleanse these demons out…
with zealous exhibitionism.
nothing that you say
can slow its drive,
even your devotion to the catechism,
it's just another mechanism
slowing down our evolution,
throw another wrench into the gears
of the peoples revolution.
From the lips and tongues
of messiahs and firebrands
comes whispers of control, restraint.
peace finally a concept
that's actually easy now to find.
Hidden in plain view,
these loyal men, of kings and coronets
reward our faith in kind.

These men in fatigues
who bark order and abuse
fade into dust
these weapons of war
crumble with rust.
The awakening of the world
of eyes, and ears and minds.
Voices loud with words of trust.
This is the end of the beginning
the beginning of the end.
The dawn of something beautiful,
the start of something new,
soak in the colours,
the aroma and the hues.
These trees we grow
from tiny seeds,
the future imperfect,
but no longer in need
ours to protect
the renaissance of Genesis.
A patch of paradise
to call my own.

Farther.

In every full persons life
is a vacuum of nothing.
Ominous silences
that make comfy inside the abyss
we call our hearts.
Abyss, I say
because never have I found
anything that can satiate
this wanton gluttony
that aches and gasps,
teeth chattering,
stomach rumbling and growling
the infallible, unfillable void
that cavernously exists
in the empty cathedral
of my heart.
The vacuum yearns,
it moans,
like a stalking, sneaky tiger.
Pawing gently
through the undergrowth.
The tree line shivering
in umber and flame.
The jungle edges in
raw, primal, hungry
becoming drunk on
the idea of you.

Untitled (II).

When you go looking
you're bound to find
those tiny fragments
of ourselves
that we leave behind.

We are over-reaching.
We are obscure, but needed.
Alive but fleeting
coddled like babes
in their wombs so bright.

Goose.

The littlest thing becomes a mountain to you.
I'm fine.
Leave the thermostat be.

It's just a goose walking over my grave.
That's what my grandmother would say...

"*Goosebumps is just a Goose walking over your grave*."

And then she'd bark that cackle she called a laugh,
all giddy as anything over her own joke.

So leave it.
Nothing but molehills here.

The arrow through the clouds.

On an unknown path,

where dragons lay

and danger strays

and darkness seeps

from crag and mire,

the uneasy crawl

of fear will linger

but through the cracks

in clouds and fog

comes hope.

Your eyes are wide

your mind on fire

the beat of your heart

makes you climb higher

as the burst of adventure

that lies in your soul

carries you forward

and makes you feel whole.
The curiosity of what
yet may be discovered
pushes like an engines piston
and punches holes
through thick grey sky
and the beam of optimism,
of blue and yellow
paints the path anew
and this ethereal arrow
lights my way.

The sprung hill.

There is provenance and wisdom in the words
"You should never go back."
Much as there is a sense of experience and a muted sadness
in the voice of the people who say it.

I had heard the words a lot recently,
from people who I trusted and loved growing up,
whom I had shared intimate secret moments
and rambunctious devil-may-care acts of thrill and terror with.

Softly whispering about the places of my youth
with the friends I shared such vivid experiences with growing up,
all of which looked back at me intently
with sadness permeating the skin around their eyes,
dark rings appearing
as soon as the words about our childhood home
leave my lips and enter their ears.

"You should not go back."
They would say,
a hand reaching out and holding my arm in tentative, sullen fashion.

"Don't go back."
They'd whisper into my own ear,
leaning in, the tang of frosty reluctance frozen to their tongue.

As is the way with stubborn men
with wild ideas of their own,
and thick warm blood coursing through cold proud veins –
I paid no difference and set out
on my way back to the land of my childhood.

Disappointment and disaster nothing but a horizon away.

Arteries.

Tendrils wrapped
and scattered
around the country.
Arteries pumping in
one direction, alone
the flow and ebb
a confusing shudder
the ripples shaking
from the bones.
Each snaking finger
of canal and river
that wriggles
through mountain
or plain or ditch,
returns again to
oceanic abandon,
turning and twisting
in whiplash wave.

The rain that lashes

the wind that rips

the sullen shower

that soaks and blankets

these sad and lonely streets.

Each river flows

away from the source,

only to crease

right back to the core.

Ocean, river, stream.

Magnificent, significant
this thump inside my chest.
Relaying blood to organs,
this engine driving self.
A creeping edge of danger
a knife slashed in the dark,
the voice that whispers quietly
and intimidates and sparks.
A sudden defibrillation,
bursts of shock and awe.
Kickstarting your decisions
and makes your brain cry "MORE."
A shadow on a cloudy day,
the flash in your periphery.
You could have sworn you were alone,
but now you aren't so sure.
The thunder-clap that precedes the storm,
the breath before the fall.
The blinding light from shooting stars
you wish you could see more.
The long held secret,
you struggle with,
that's bursting to get out.
The choked back scream
when you need stealth,
the empty coffers

your only wealth,
these pennies and these farthings.
You wish to be a hawk, my dear,
but you prove more of a starling.
The shooting stars,
the meteorites, that burn up on re-entry.
You call yourself a warrior,
but you're really more a sentry.
Standing guard, holding the line,
protector and defender.
You count yourself a starter,
when you are really more an ender.
The flickering flame
that lights the fuse,
that burns down to the powder.
The explosion in the dead of night
the hand upon the shoulder.
The crack upon the window pane,
that blows in broken
in the cold, and freezes in your veins.
the touch of Death, who strokes your brow,
reassures you, tells you how -
this is really not the end.
Who guides you gently
into the night,
your hand in his you wander.
Step by step, inch by inch,
until the the light is all you see,
the world now blurred and empty.

The afterlife your haven,
Heaven now your shelter.
You conquered all you tackled,
you won more than you lost,
the life you lived an inspiration,
to every creed and nation.
And now to silent restfulness
you find yourself a-slumbering.
a final place to rest your head,
a pillow made of rock.
The noise, the sound,
the peace and fury,
muted, fading too black.
The rope goes loose,
the pressure slack.
We know you were once here,
the sad fact is - that after this,
you are never coming back.
No ghost, no spirit,
no spectral ghoul.
21 grams of mystery,
a little slice of history,
now you are a fable.
The only way you will remain
as folklore, rumour, fairy tale -
a character inside a book
that you no longer author.
The final pages
long obscured,

no longer son or daughter.
Your name lives on in legend,
a legacy remembered.
Live hard, live free,
love long and pure…
Because these days,
for good or bad,
are always short in number.

Wicker-kid plays with matches.

Grab hold - get over
look for something new.
Hold tight, remember
these flames look good on you.

You're gold - I'm sober
this shine is new on you.
Let go, surrender
theses flames burn fast and true.

Lick spittle fire's friend
light the fuse
watch to the end.
Soon we'll be a headline on the news.

Scorched Earth policies,
Ash hides atrocities.
Skeletons are charred
and shallow in their graves.

This wicked kid,
this wicker-kid
prone to combustion,
and flirting with the flame.

Cody Jarrett was right.

Isolate, inoculate.
Curb this spread of germs.
Warfare on a microscopic scale,
viral particles underneath nails.
Invisible fronts, advancing eagerly,
infestation unseen,
the city falls to silent terror,
the likes of which we've seldom seen.

Welcome to the year 3000.
Lockdown 408.
The levels of idiocy no different
from the last 800 years.

No more trees, no water clean,
no air remains, just dust and dreams.
A faded memory of what we used to be,
a shroud of nostalgia,
choking back our tears.
Deaf, dumb and blind,
we still instagram our day,
this now is the only fragment of the past,
that the future clings to
in stubborn tradition.

We hold the phone aloft,

like a dozy mirror,
Blind to what we have reflecting back at us.
We cannot see the picture,
but we know we've nailed the pose.

No more a human race,
now a human crawl.
Edging toward the cliff face,
plummeting toward ten thousand likes.

So much influence,
before we hit those rocks.
Top of the world, Ma.

Look at me, I made it.

Female of the species.

"She's harmless"
they said.
But nothing with teeth is ever truly harmless.
Your nerves will always be expectant of the bite.

"She's friendly"
they said.
But nothing hiding daggers behind their backs,
sharpened and dripping with poison,
will ever be your friend.

There is always a danger
of being the sheath for tooth or dagger
someday in the future, my friend.

The female of the species
never truly sleeps.
Instead they plot, and simmer,
primed and ready to pounce.

They will draw a litre,
if you even tease them with an ounce.

Don't get me wrong,
I love them all.
The female of the species.
Yet, i'm a male,

so predisposed
to idiocy and failure.
Mistakes they come a-tumbling,
regardless best intention.

So my neck is always ready
for the sinking in of teeth,
to draw the thin weak blood,
that pulses underneath.

And to this,
I admit,
I probably deserve it.
Because I listened to you stupidly,
when you said -
"She is a friend"
And instead I wandered aimlessly,
toward my lonely end.

Marie Celeste.

Well it's easy to see
when you rock the boat
you make waves.
So why not come back to the shore,
we can all talk,
and you'll stay.
It's the right thing now,
for all of us to do.
We can make you safe,
we can provide for you.

Well it's easy to see,
that we aren't in a place
to be friends.
But please tell me this,
is this really how
you saw it end?

So come back to port,
we can talk this through.
We have shelter and food,
we'll look after you.

Please tell me that you will stay.

Well it's easy to see,
that we devastated the town
to no end.
Safe harbour or not,
we are too proud to be friends.

We scorched earth and root,
we cut the pipes and we stood,
on the ashes of all that we could.

This is a petty end,
part of a selfish trend.
We could have been so great,
instead, we separate.

Please tell me that you'll be safe.

Well, i'm sad to see
that you sailed off alone
with no oars.
The tide gripped your ship,
and bore you south,
distant shores.

There are monsters there.
Rocks and sirens galore.
with your rudder gone,
and no canons aboard.
I don't know how you will fare.

Well, it's been ten years now -
that you sailed off alone from this coast.
no sign of your ship,
no sign of your flag or your ghost.
Just a dull memory.
or what could have been.

I hope that the tide was your friend.

But mostly, dear -
I hope I never see you again.

I am closing the chapter,
I am closing the book.
A final full stop,
as I admit to myself,
this is at last, the end.

And admit to myself,
Despite all of my hopes,
despite all of my dreams.

You were never really my friend.

A frantic flash of fiction.

I cannot find the words.

The verbs, the nouns, the adjectives…
they escape me.
I am blank.
I cannot structure,
I have no path,
no map toward the end.
Sentences escape me,
and metaphors are gone.
I am fearful of the void
that exists inside my mind.

Names have packed their bags,
and vacationed from my memory.
I cannot recall grammar,
or how to parse a line or three.

The whirlpool of nothingness,
the panic of dull thought,
the story is now loose, but I am not in control.
I try to wrangle, wrestle, to corral it back to shape…
to drag it screaming back in line
but I have no control to take.

This is a frenzy.
A frantic flash of fiction.
But it is writing me.
no longer am I master,
but now a slave to my own words.

A matter of style and poise.

Lost in the clouds, she finally realised that falling was the same as flying.

The only difference was technique,
A matter of style and poise.

It's easy to fall… you just let go.
But to fly while you fall is a skill.
A twist of the hips, a stretch of the arm.
An elegance and fearlessness that so many seem without.

She realised that in falling,
you are poetry in motion… as long as you decide to be such.
There is an ease to falling,
an innocence.
A naivety.

No such naivety in flying.
To soar, catching those thermal drafts, and taking wing to the wind,
that requires a balance of mind and body that is dormant and sleeping
while you fall.

The switch is primal,
the trigger panic,
but soon, if you allow it you will be skimming clouds, tasting the fresh
clean air of the stratosphere and bathing in the sunlight.

A radiant, bright baptism.

When thinking of my childhood, I think of...

Horse chestnut trees,
and broken ladders.
Collecting conkers from high topped branches,
plummeting to Earth in a fit and flurry,
smashing down on branches
whiplashed skin and muscle
as the ground draws up to meet me.

I think of barbed wire fences
cutting through my clothes and skin,
as I run straight into them
panicked and bruised.
The fall leaving me dazed and dozy;
my faculties frenetic.

I think of go-karts careening
down the hills that line our little world.
Gutters and ditches our only escape
as we swerve cars and vans,
hitting speeds unheard of
for a twelve year old.
No helmets or knee-pads,
no safety gear as we speed.

My childhood was open fields
and dense rings of trees.

It was springs and streams
and danger and recklessness.
It was getting lost for hours
in meadows around a prison.

It was always being home for tea
before the street lights go dull orange,
fizzing ever so bright.
Of fairies and of ghosts,
and things that bump into the night.

But mostly it was happiness,
unrepentant laughter.
Of friends who would of marched to war,
had I ever asked them.
Of bows and arrows made by fathers,
and jumpers laid for goalposts.

Of breaking into garages
and fights that were disasters.
Of football games in blazing sun,
of first kisses on cricket greens,
concrete tennis courts
and bleeding knees.

Of adventure and stupidity,
and falling, falling, falling from those monstrous conker trees.

To do list.

These demands upon my time are testing.
Barely able to scrape together
a single minute to get rested.
Anxiety is pulsing,
but the voices are all blasting -
Demanding that I dedicate my everything
to this frantic grafting.

It's crafty - the way that life
demands from you
but barely pays the fee I'm asking.
Tasking me to get it done,
but never for a second
considering the damage done,
on mental health and piece of mind,
of closing eye and sleeping tight,
without thinking of the fight
that this task is bringing
every fucking day and every fucking night.

I am not being paid enough
to tolerate this shit.
Staggering to comprehend
the never-ending financial hit
upon my tiny wage and salary.
Try in vain to scrimp and save,
but barely have a penny
that I can pull out on a rainy day.

Fuck this bullshit.

This routine I seem embroiled in.
This facade of a career
that I have found myself
well and truly trapped within.
Earning a pittance, not a benefit in sight,
as all the bosses take off
on holidays to locales so bright.
Driving cars that cost more
than everything I own,
whilst here I am, counting penny's,
whilst in debt I drown.

I am just a slave,
to a wage that doesn't pay.
Forever mutely nodding,
as no one listens to what I say.
Just another number in a ledger,
just a name within the books.
Try and find the greener grass,
always disappointed where I look.

An artist or a writer,
an ambition to create.
But sadly these fine fancies
do not put food upon the plate.
A thousand poems,
a million words, or paint upon the canvas,
may be nice to look at,
but don't put a roof above my head.
If I carry on feasting
on all this free exposure,
i'll soon be pretty dead.

But there it is, lunch is done,
my hour now is over,

So back to the grind, handcuffed to desk,
Emails, they need an answer,
a billion stupid questions,
from every direction,
and not a single one,
will mean a fucking thing.
An experiment in monotony,
aimed solely at frustrating me.

To end the day, we commute,
stuck in standstill traffic,
swearing under breath.
If I carry on this burden,
this toil and this torture,
regardless of the hours spent,
it will surely lead to death.
Another day, another dollar -
or so the saying goes.
Staring over garden fences,
forever fucking jealous of
how my neighbours garden grows.

TikTok.

You're so transparent
I can see all of your
levers and gears working.
Grinding to a halt
because of the
muck that you keep raking.

Throwing reputations,
torn in tatters,
on the fires that you are stoking.
Choking back the tears,
from this inferno
you have smoking.
A smouldering of sorrow
from the ashes of what's broken.

Sing a song o'six pence
may I never tell a lie.
Caught between a rock,
and the fire in the sky.
The clouds are plumes of poison,
the grass is grey and acrid
the result of all the bridges
that you seem intent on burning.

The haunted shore.

There are ghosts within these ruins,
these ruins of my heart.
A crumbling castle of reflection,
experience, attraction.
Caustic weather, dissolves and batters,
these fragments of the things that matter.
Leaving me a husk of the man I wish I was.

Fingernails are broken,
fractured, damaged, dulled.
Scratching myself back
to a place I should belong.
A heavy burden tires me,
the time it takes has loosened
all the strings that held me up.
Nothing but a puppet now,
slouched and masterless.

There are mermaids in the distance,
but they bare their teeth
when you approach.
The rocks - jagged, dangerous,
the risk is just enough
to pay off in some hard reward,
some treasure or some folly.
I'll take the gamble foolishly,
my fate a random playing card,

plucked out of the deck.
Upon the well worn chopping block,
I happily lay my neck.

There are ghouls within the wreckage,
Banshees wailing
for some past horror,
shrieking sadness, distress and sorrow.
Songs to which your heart will shatter.
Your will then bends to idle chatter,
and all upon the pyre bright,
your soul will burn
upon the Earth to blight.

Shorts & Prose.

Sharing stories.

Written for the 2016 Stratford Upon Avon Literary Festival Short Story Competition.

(It didn't win.)
(I'm not bitter. Honest.)

Though the teeth chattered inside their mouths, no words escaped their lips. Just a silence lingering upon the chilly air.
Their hands busily worked the bags open. Zips whipped, canvas flapped wide and lean. Those frost-bitten hands pulling leather-bound tomes from deep within.

They shared the books amongst the room; the words inside irrelevant. The contents meaningless. Any power they had in poetry long since lost, any poignancy and purpose in the words lost generations before.

The books now were good for one purpose and one purpose only. One man took a stick of charred wood from the bag and scrawled upon the floor a crude pictogram of flame. Two more men nodded sagely, and calloused rough hands began to rip the pages from the book and drop the littered shreds into a large tin can.

A matchstick dropped, and the pages became nothing more than tinder to the flame. The light began to shimmer and shake in licks and lances of heat.

There was a silence.
Nothing but the feint crackle of fire and slow sucked whoosh of paper folding to ash. It was so loud, being so quiet.
Every creak, every breath, every slight movement groaned in agonising, screaming levels of volume.
The room alive and shaking with the weakest, smallest movement.

Snapping and crackling the fire burned to embers. Shadows cast weakly on the wallpaper, dancing figures flickered and fluttered as the flames fanned to short licks in the timber.
The darkness was setting in earlier and earlier, and the cold had

come tandem alongside it. The wind tap-tap-tapped the weak windows and the single pane glass groaned and shuddered as the outside came to call. The view was nothing more than an inky blue void of landscape. Nothing stood out. Nothing made itself known save the bleak empty vista of the field and the dilapidated cornrows beyond.

The boy sat in the corner tinkering with the remnants of the broken radio, his back not quite to the rest of the group, but isolated all the same. His small candle providing scant illumination to help in his efforts – he toiled on regardless. Nimble hands working the wires and the screws, the plastic and metal and the internal components in expert fashion.

Nothing came from the radio; its silence was all but deafening. But he carried on regardless trying to repair the wretched thing.

The first man rose from the bag of books, he reached inside and took a final one out. Chewing on a toothpick; light bites and nibbles, a sweet suckling noise with each rotation of the stick from left of his mouth to right.

He watched the boy in the corner, fidgeting with the relic of the machine they had found on the road, the boy drawing in the snow a box with circles on the left and right, a rectangle in the center, and a handle. The parts and components picked up and put inside a plastic carrier bag they had found snagged on a tree.

Carried proudly from location to location and slowly but surely remade bit by bit at each stop.

The man idly flipped a coin in between his fingers – the silver disc dancing from knuckle to knuckle, a fluid, warm shimmer of metal that caught the light and shone an echo onto the wall above the boy's head.

The boy stopped his tinkering and he looked up at the light fluttering around on the wall, his bright green eyes following the darting jagged shapeless light as it moved at random around the wall, then, spinning his head toward the man, he raised a single finger, bringing it high and placed it on his mouth.
He closed his eyes and shook his head, ever so gently, a subtle – almost invisible gesture.

No noise – but a clear order to hush.

The man stopped his idling. Stopped his tricksy coin play.
He held his hand up in a solemn apologetic *"ok."* And put a finger to his lips himself, his young features went a blank passive shape as he closed his eyes and nodded to the boy.
The boy didn't respond or reply, instead, his hands went to his radio and sleek, tiny fingers continued to toil around on the dial, his other hand continuing to fumble with wires and mechanisms in the back of the pulled apart device.

Attention quite somewhere else entirely.

The man watched the others in the room, gently rubbing their hands together and blowing quietly to warm cold skin, gloveless hands floating above the open flames, rubbing some warmth into the bones beneath, no-one talking, no one making any noise apart from restless shuffle of clothing as they adjusted themselves against walls and corners where they huddled and rested.

The house was quiet, astonishingly, agonisingly so.
The silence so loud it screamed.

A little girl looked up at him as he padded in gentle steps toward the kitchen and the backdoor. She took his gloveless hand in her mittened one and she smiled up at him. He smiled back, passed her the book and watched contentedly as she eagerly ripped out pages and threw them into the fire can, he smiled and blew her a calm, loving kiss and waved it down to her. He took his charred stick and drew a hand with one thumb raised, and beside it, a crude drawing of puckered lips - the girl looked down at the charcoal scribbles, and held her hands close to her heart. She smiled wide and gummy at the man, nodding her understanding and appreciation.

The front two teeth in her mouth, at the top, missing, her smile a wide gappy-toothed grin that provoked a wider smile in return from the man. He looked back at her as she hugged closer to her mother in the dining room, pulled under a blue shawl being used as a cover. Dropping more pages into the can. The flames growing, the light glowing, the warmth clear and welcome.

The man strode to the back door, still smiling at the girls smile. He pulled the door open and suddenly, the quiet, calm world was roaring with the wind and the growing blizzard outside.
Winds that howled and whistled in bare branched trees and dark, navy skies.

Winds that growled stories into the night air for mountains and roads, forests and woodland to listen to.

One of the rough handed men came outside and joined him. He clapped the younger man on the shoulder and he turned and gently smiled a welcome. The rough handed man offered him a cigarillo – a hand-rolled, ugly cigarette. Thin and colourless – The younger man appreciatively took it, dragged back and exhaled a tendril of smoke to the sky. Blue-grey, it spiralled and drew stories into the navy canvas above – pictures of Viking ships, mingling with the snow, it painted a fairy tale all of its own creation, before dispersing into nothingness, and leaving only the sky - dark blue and daunting.

The rough handed man took a nearby broken branch and drew in the snowy ground a picture of a boy, then a version of the radio, next to this he drew a face – eyes looking skyward, a hand below the mouth holding the chin quizzically.
Questioning.
The young man gazed back inside, and saw the smiling girl, and he elicited a small, gentle grin once again – beyond her, in the far corner he saw the boy busily pottering away. With his charred stick he knelt down and drew a hand, two fingers raised and crossed, next to this he drew a face with hands pressed together in front of it, eyes closed. Praying.

The older man drew below this a face with wide-open eyes, a line for a mouth – an exasperated, unimpressed expression. Next to this he drew a pair of crossed fingers as well.

The younger man nodded.

He clasped the rough handed man on the shoulder, they smiled at each other and stood in the snowstorm, wind blowing their hair, cigarillos burning down to the tip, smoke coming from their mouths as they dragged back deep breaths. The silence between them only interrupted by the howl of the wind. The creak and crunch of the snow as it became heavier and thicker and – *then* – a burst of static from inside the house.

Both men spun on their heels, cigarillos dropping to the white ground, a fizzle of the burnt end snuffing out in the cold.
They looked at each other, then to the house, before the younger man burst back through the door and paced in wide hurried steps toward the room where the boy was sat.

The people in the house had huddled in terror to corners, grasping each other tight; children hidden behind a line of men, each ready to attack if needed.
The man saw the toothless girl and she looked terrified. She raised a single finger accusatorially to the boy, who sat silent, his back to the rest of the room – no longer tinkering. No longer toiling on the machine. Now, sat with his head at an angle of satisfied candour regarding the device.
Cross-legged, his hands on his knees, and his head rest slightly upon them.

The young man, and the rugged handed man trudged into the room, and looked down at the boy; his face barely lit now in the waning candlelight.
The boy looked up at them and smiled.
With his finger into the dusty floor, he drew the radio again. Then, a

hand - making the "OK" sign, of a ring between thumb and forefinger and three raised fingers.

From the radio, static burst in shocking stabs of white noise.
The men put their hands over their ears and looked at each other, the people in the other room, and then the boy.
The child smiled up at the men, and then raised a finger to his lips and gestured for them to take their hands away.

They did, and what happened next chilled and excited them to their marrow, as the static gave way, no longer jagged, stabbing, sharp fractured sound.
Instead, a slight, muffled hiss of a steady channel, and - quietly at first, but getting louder - something else.

The boy turned toward the radio, and said in a whisper, his voice a muffled, muted moan, a clear sentence.

"It was the best of times; it was the worst of times..."

The words repeated on the radio.
Once, then again, then over and over.

Not that these people knew what words were.
Like the books, the language was alien and dead, futile and lost.
Generations of people who had only pictures and pictograms to talk with. No need for sounds and language. No matter – here – the radio spoke.
The first words in their lifetime.
Sounds of the past communicating to them, and letting them know that it would be ok... That they were alright.

"It was the best of times; it was the worst of times…"

Language reborn.
Words.
Such delicious, scary, wonderful words…

The boy turned and looked at the men, and a wide smile on his lips, he said clearly – to them and the rest of the world –

"It was the best of times; it was the worst of times…"

And outside, as within, a new dawn bravely broke in the not so distant horizon. A new day, a new world to go with it, made from lost, yet familiar things – now, rediscovered and repeating over and over and over.

Stories shared across the static.

Found again, at last.

3:47am conversations with God. Pt.1

Based on actual events.*

* This is a probably lie.

"Now I lay me down to sleep, pray the lord my soul to ke…"

"I wouldn't bother."

"Is that you again God?"

"Yup… As ever."

"Jesus Christ man, what do you want now…?"

"Just came to say hello, brother."

"It's 3.47 in the AM, could you not skip tonight? I'm tired…"

"No can do Compadre. Time waits for no man… Nor God. It seems."

"OOOOOOHHHHH!"
"AHHHHHH!"

"Fine… Can you do me a favour though and ask the host incarnate to keep it down? I have neighbours…"

"Sorry. My Corporeal host have a taste for the dramatic."

"OOOOOOHHHHH!"
AAAHHHH…"

"Can-it guys… he's not in the mood."

"… oh."

"Sorry. What can I say? – Apparently, he has neighbours…"

"Fine… ingrate!"

"Hey guys… there's no need for that...
seriously. thats's just rude.
God, do they not bother you?"

"I barely notice them anymore."

"Alright for you, I suppose, but with my soft human squishy mind sometimes I find it hard to differentiate between voices, harp orchestras and the tingling sensation felt when God talks direct at me without aid of the Megatron."

"Metatron. Megatron was a robot that turned into a gun, Metatron is an angel that acts as my PA."

"*Whatever… You get the picture.*"

'I certainly do Son. After all… I'm God.
GOD.
Capital *G*. Capital *OD*."

"As you say... repeatedly, over and over again.
Every time a flood happens and a village is washed down hill toward oblivion or a school shooting occurs, and a dozen or more children are reported massacred at the hands of one of their former friends or an earthquake in some Guatemalan village that devastates countless miles of shanty shacks…

As excuses go mate, it's getting tiresome."

"Well… Sorry you feel that way.
Sorry I'm not Satan and his oh-so-fancy jibber jabber about rock'n'roll, cocaine and the movie industry…
Sorry I'm over here trying to work for a living."

"Pah! Work… sure.

What are the rates of pay like? Do you have any spaces going for recruitment?
Can I get involved on the ground floor?"

"Sarcasm will get you nowhere as a species you know?"

"I know… I know…
You know I am only kidding.
And you need to lighten up about Satan, he's a good bloke really.
It's nice to let of some steam with him sometimes.
You are a bit serious you know?"

"Serious? Serious How?"

"You just seem a bit self-obsessed sometimes.
It's ALWAYS all about you.
What you achieved in six days. What you did for us all in creation.
How wonderful a gardener you are.
Preaching about how you invented water flow dynamics, temperature alignment and volcanic mass management.
You're not a gloater, you just seem very keen to big up your own work…
ALL THE TIME"

"I never thought about it that way."

"Hey, it's fine.
You know. If I had built everything we see in seven days
- six if you don't count the half day at the end -
Well, I would be a bit boasty as well.
But sometimes, it's all a little You, You, You.
You know what I mean?"

"It's certainly something to think about."

"Good. Personal growth is an important thing…

Look, I hate to sound like a moaning myrtle -
Would you mind turning down the Halo as well, it's hurting my eyes a bit, I have fears of you burning out my retinas."

"Good idea. Don't want that.
I forget I have it half the time, if I am honest.
Eyes, Brother, eyes are a serious business."

"Serious business eh?"

"For sure! Making them, a piece of piss.
Fixing them after they get screwed up?
Well, even I am stumped. Sometimes, just sometimes my son, you kind of just stumble into these things and then you're stuck to leaving them to figure themselves out afterwards.
Not worth the bother of playing around with the lovely little things, you'll only cause a mischief.
I mean, just look at duck-billed platypi...
Genuinely, I have no personal idea what happened there, they just… were. So I left them.

…They seem happy enough.

Better to just leave them to their own devices."

"So why are you here then Boss?
Why should I not bother with my evening prayers?
I thought this stuff was like food for you or something?
Swallowing down the worship and tribute"

"Yes… usually… But, not tonight.
Tonight, *everything* changes."

"Changes? How so?"

"You should probably make yourself comfy, Son.
I have something pretty serious to tell you.

You see – hmmm… Where to start?"

*"How about the beginning?
This sounds like you need to get a lot of your chest… Shall I put the kettle on?"*

"Not really in the mood for tea.
Ha! It's funny you should ask me though.
Let me tell explain.
You see.
The thing is - and I don't mean this personally…
I really don't brother.
But...
well.

You were an accident."

"I'm an accident?! Me??!"

"Oh goodness no… Not you YOU.
I meant the royal YOU.
Humans… the old Homo Sapes…
big accident. Total mistake.

"Oh…Ok. Elaborate."

"Basically, there I was playing around with the stars and the planets and the celestial gasses, and what would you know – as these things happen, boredom sets in.
There I am floating around, playing silly buggers with balls of ferocious, explosive gas and chunks of ice-bitten frosty snowflakes,

when I realise, 'There must be more to everything than this?'"

"Perfectly understandable. What did you do?"

"Well, I went off on a wander.
It's amazing really, in the early days I was so busy doing everything single handedly - before the Host came along - that I was knocking stuff out with no thought or record keeping. All the admin. Y'know. Masse's of the stuff.
But after a while it all gets so busy and so hectic I have no idea what's bloody what and I decide -
'That's that! I need a break'
So I down tools and stage a one man strike against myself.
Pack a small bag and off I wander amongst the stars and portals of my universe I had literally just created.
The thing is Son..
I may be the creator of everything and I may know all of everything in my creation, but – and here's the thing - it gets awful chaotic at times in my head with the noises and voices and sounds of the omniverse cascading in and out of my almost incomprehensibly massive mind, that I more often than not just – you know…
Ignore them.
Kind of phase it all out…
And so therein lays our problem."

"Problem? We have a problem?"

"Oh yes son!
A Huge one.
You see…
Earth… Well, Earth was one of the last things I worked on, lovely greens and blues - always been partial to greens and blues, but when I left on my travels, I didn't tidy up after myself.
There's Earth, right where I left it, far too close to the oven…
Sorry... Not oven...

Sun!
Whatever you wish to call it. And, like a cup with a little tea in the bottom, left on a windowsill in sunlight, things start to take over and do their own thing.
Mould…
Humans… The like."

"*Mould?...*
Humans?...
Are you saying that….
Wait a second. Wh… What are you saying?"

"What I think I am trying to say is…
We're here.
Then we're gone.
But nature, she carries on.
You humans were an accident. And as much as I wish I could sit here and take all the credit that is given to me in the books…

"*Books? You mean - The Bible??*"

"Well… Primarily, yes, *The Bible.*
You may have waltzed around like some free-range chicken for a hundred thousand million millennia, but, in my frame of reference, I left you for thirty seconds so I could go off and do me for half a minute, and look what you've done to the place?
War, famine, billions of dead, diseases I had never even heard of before. Hatred, religious persecution, suicide bombs?
SUICIDE BOMBS?? - I mean, Christ on a bike. Where did you come up with that??
The whole thing is a shambles.
And even though it will only take me a matter of an hour or so to fix the lot, that's not the point.
You've made a right mess, and no mistake.

So…
Despite our chats, and a long ponder and evaluation of the species as a whole and the world in general…
I have come to the conclusion that I am…
Erm…
Well…"

"Go on…"

"I'm ending it.
I am going to end it, and I am starting again.
I am - to use a metaphor you might understand better –
'Cleaning the cup'.
'I'm bleaching the mug'…
'I am degreasing my soup bowl.'
Bye Bye Mould…
Bye Bye bacteria, hello shiny clean, blue and green ball of loveliness again."

"So…"

"So."

"So… you are telling me that… This is the end?
That you are here to take me to heaven?"

"Oh goodness no.
HA! Heaven…
And have you run around my house grubbying up the place?
No No No! Ha!
Would bleach invite streptococcus in for tea? I don't think so!!"

"Nice, i'm a germ now… Seems harsh.
So what are you saying… That this is it? End a chapter. Weep. Start again."

"Well… I don't know if I will weep."

"You're telling me that you are ending the world and I am not coming with you to heaven?"

"Yes.
That is what is happening, but when you put it like that, you do make it sound like a buzzkill.
I mean, at least I am telling you straight to your face.
After all our chats, I thought it would be good to be honest.
After all, you helped me come to the decision! If not for you, this dirty cup may have just sat there and gotten even dirtier!
I really hoped that by sharing this information with you that we would be cool… Are we not cool?"

"Not really.
Truth be told, I feel sick…
I feel nauseous. I'm gonna hurl…"

"Oh… Well this next bit will really not help then…

"Next bit?"

"Yeah…"

"What?"

"I'm doing it tonight,"

"God?"

"Yes brother…?"

"You're an asshole."

"Well… Now who is being harsh?
I'm an arsehole am I?
Well - explains a lot… I did make you in my own image…"

***

Fibro and me.
(Or "1327")

Written for my darling cousin Vix Dutton –
Based upon her title, as a commission via my website.

A lot of research and a wonderful amount of feedback from people who have lived with Fibro-myalgia went into the writing of this addition, I am elated that people found something inside this story that touches on personal levels.

Suffice to say, I'm really proud of this one.

Waking up was never usually a problem for Vanessa, waking was generally a pretty easy, simple process that anyone could do. After all, you just opened your eyes and it was done.

No, waking wasn't a problem.
But everything before and after was, and the problem was only getting worse.

Last night was a pretty easy night as they went. Bed by 10pm, the street lights outside far enough away on the main road that the warm soda orange glow was only subtle behind the thin cream curtains on her bare magnolia walls.
The sound of the city was always there, of course, but it was a bare whisper this evening. The ambulance and police sirens were still singing their night song on the air, but the city made this as mellifluous as the birds after a few weeks, and Vanessa zoned it out as she always did.

The song inside her bones was dull tonight as well. Its high-pitched banshee cry was muted and only a low murmuring drone. So, she had gone to bed with a glass of cold water and a soothed head, and slept the majority of the evening.

God knows this is not always the case; not always was this simple process so easy.

She lay down painting the images of dreams on her ceiling, watching passing cars swash colour and trails of light from one corner of her bedroom to the other as they disappeared down her road. Headlights blazing. Engines revving a goodbye of sorts to the evening.
As she did this, the dull drone inside her became a more prominent throb, a fuzzy ache, but still was not anywhere as near as it may have been on previous evenings.

The covers pulled higher, and the slight waft of breeze from the cracked window acted in duality with each other, and Vanessa drifted off to sleep.

Her dreams were colourful flashes of images, and sounds, visions and blurs. No details that startled or lingered.
Just a mash of sensations and warmth.

She slept. Her breathing a pulsing sigh and moan of relief. Silent. Calm. Gentle relief. Soak it in before the morning was there again and the drone had cascaded into a heavy and angry burst of aching and angry hammer blows throughout her entire body.

The wake-up call of the Fibro.

On unsteady feet, Vanessa forced herself to sitting, and her eyes wet with tears, unexpected and sudden, she rubbed her knees and elbows, stroked gently on her own shoulders and collarbone, and then round her neck and lower back.
The pain was a constant roadmap of throbs, pangs and stabs.
Every inch of her body hurt, even her eyes.
The illness had come in the night with vengeance and fury and now she was awake to its grasp again.

Vanessa slowly, with a meandering puppet-like movement that looked delicate and fragile raised herself to her feet and then shuffled toward the bathroom, where she looked at herself in the full length, brass framed mirror – taking in the bend of her back, the twist of her hip, the clutch of her hands wrapped around her stomach. And she cried again.

The pain was a constant chatter now. Gone was the whisper in her ear, quiet and calm. Instead, an amplified drill sergeant shouted and screamed at her every step.
And so, to the shower she shuffled further. Turning on the hot and cold taps, and slowly, shedding her night shirt to the floor, she stepped inside naked and aching to allow the warm water to pound

the flesh and bring slight calmness.

This illness was a silent – but noisy – partner that walked every step with her. Sometimes (though rarer and rarer the times were) it tiptoed behind, holding its mouth, except for the occasional giggle or guffaw.

More often, despite the drugs and the painkillers and the constant referrals to doctors and hospitals and medical Centre's – the shadow was an angry, loud mouthed braggart who spoke often and out of turn. Who prodded and poked when ignored and who always had to make its presence felt and known.

Vanessa never considered herself single.
Though she was.
She was in a relationship with her illness. And it was abusive, and uneven, and hectic and violent. But there were no shelters or helplines she could call. Instead, she took the pills, took a delicate and soft version of yoga, tried aimlessly to harness the world around to lessen her burden, and lived in constant fear of the partner she never asked for, who drove a wedge in her life that pushed her further and further away from her goals and aspirations and more often than not dictated her schedule, life and every waking moment.

The water fell hard and heavy on her skin; ricocheting off in every direction as she stood idle, head in hands and cried to herself about the pain.
The pain in turn – *ever the gentleman* - mocked and laughed and prodded and poked and harassed and did not let up, not once.

Her joints cracked and hurt when she raised her arm to rub the shower lotion onto her skin. She ignored it as bad as it was, as best as she could, and lathered down to allow her skin a wonderful moment of clarity amongst the pain, as the lotion basked and soaked in.

Then she rinsed stood still under the waterfall of the shower, and watched the suds swirl and rotate down the outlet hole.
Soapy twirls and flailing patterns that looked like creamy, pearlescent dragons swam and flirted with the plug before disappearing in silent bursts of light and dark.

She stepped out, drips running down her body. Each drip leaving a trail of tingling sensation as it ran on her sensitive and brittle skin.
In a thrall of a sensation overload, she sat gently on the toilet – lid down – using it as a still, wrapped in a warm, thick, fluffy white towel.

At these worst times, she focused beyond the angry throb of her bones and tried to leave her body and exist only in her mind. Inventing worlds and scenarios. Escape hatches into a new place away from the world; concentrating all her many tingling cells on one place that existed only in her mind and subconscious.
And slowly but surely, in front of her, one such door manifested and became real.

A bright Red door, with a number in bold brass – 1327 – emblazoned upon it. Vanessa was still sat, her eyes closed, her arms wrapped about her clutched in towel, errant strands of water running lines of moisture on her pale skin, made red from the showers heat.
And from the centre and core of her, a new arm grew, and reached out.
Its hand folded on the door handle of the red door, that grew as if from the air itself, and a being of light and of innocent wonder stretched out of Vanessa's chest and stepped through the pulled open door.

There was suddenly two Vanessa's.
The one sat, in pain and silence, gritted teeth harshly biting back

sobbed tears, hugging herself and concentrating hard.
The other a luminous being of sparkling quality, an aspect of patience and total calm in her eye.
She wore a thin fizzing veil of electric, upon her feet were square toed dancing shoes, and she had her hair in a tight bun, her face made up as though a swan was hiding behind the woman's visage.

She pulled the door open, and stepped out of the naked Vanessa, the vulnerable Vanessa, the pained Vanessa, and stepped through the door into the world the real Vanessa had created in her mind.

Here we were.
A being of the heart and a room from the mind, an escape hatch and a fleeting universe free of pain and full of joy, love, calm and abandon.
The Vanessa built of light smiled as she stepped through, on gentle tip-toes in fancy fashion to the middle of a large white floor, circled by giant stained glass windows, the panes made of light blues and ambers, yellows and pinks – a pastel world of muted hues and bright effervescence.

On sprung heels and dainty toes, Vanessa-of-light danced and pirouetted and swooped, her arms and legs stretching to fantastic lengths and shapes..
Long, lithe and beautiful.
Dancing amongst chairs and tables assembled of nothing but fine and solid mist and light.

The room was full of faint, tinkling music, like a music memory box had been opened. And the dancer moved in between the chairs and tables, and flared back into the empty dance floor, and spun kicks and bended knee pranced jumps and tip-toed steps into vast swinging and spinning circles.

Her body was a force of beautiful nature, at one with the vast expanse of the room, her breath a controlled and rhythmic sigh that moved in line with the music, each step and movement a beat

of the music box tinkle.
Her body a machine of order – alive and wonderful with beauty and grace.

The seated, real world Vanessa smiled. The pain throbbed back against the memory and the thought she fixated on inside her minds eye. The red door no more real than the room of light or the dancer version of her self.
But the manifestation of calm and repose.
Her way of hypnotising beyond the ache inside.
Beyond the pain that lingered and beyond the day-to-day ritual of smiling grit-toothed through the pain, the discomfort, the torture.

Vanessa lived this life every day.

The pain would come and go, the ache would grow and wane, and the torturous throb in her bones and muscles would linger for hours, days and weeks. Despite this, inside her existed a vast continent of a world in which she could tumble and fall and block out the real world if only for a few minutes a day.

Inside her, a dancer lived, made of light and hope and energy, and which was free of the pain and the noise.
Her world was one of light and dance and the brief, beautiful tinkle of the memory box. The lid opened and any one of the small red doors with brass numbers appeared and came to fleeting existence, the dancer could open the portal and fall into a new world, tumbling into the dance, for as long as was needed.

The Vanessa-of-Light and the Vanessa-of-the-real two sides of the same coin, both existing because of the other, and each working toward the same brief moment of light and love and calm.

The pain would always be here, but so would these doors and rooms of light. The pain allowed these moments of breathing and calm repose, it did not punish or begrudge the momentary tumbles into fantasy.

Indeed…

Pain did not like its job, but was trapped in an employment of life rather than desire, and though it resented itself for hurting this beautiful woman so, it smiled when the red doors appeared, and it was proud and loving of its host.
It loved Vanessa in its own strange way… both the being of light and its host body. Those doors, and the world beyond, they gave pain a meaning and purpose and an ache of its own.
The world in strange and wonderful syncopation.
The synchronicity of pain, love, light, darkness – all one and the same.

For one brief and dazzling moment, the being of flesh and the being of light, the calmness and the absence of pain, and the throbbing and aching that lived in her bones – all of them – were one and the same.
And the universe was alive.

Bright, darkness.
Dull, shadowy light.
Loud silence.
Silent cacophony.

It made no sense, but, it made perfect sense.

So, for the door and the brass numbers and the outstretched arm of the being of light, and the pause of the real for the fantasy beyond the threshold.

Pain smiled for Vanessa.

This was life, after all, neither fair nor unfair. It wasn't as binary and simple as these two opposites.
Life was a ball of confusing and wonderful possibilities, that coalesced and tumbled in elegant chaos, no one could control it, but sometimes it took shape in the most poignant and wonderful ways.
Vanessa was a being of extreme poles – relaxation and pain bending

and kissing, light and dark mixing into new hues of life and colour, fantasy and reality dancing in a wide white hall with darkened corners, adorable kisses planted on slender necks and elegant looks of love and nervous energy.

Such was life.

Vanessa dried herself of the final few droplets from the shower, and slowly, the being of light neatly and warmly climbed back inside the doorway of her heart where she lived. With a gentle sigh the real Vanessa - the being of pain and life and love - walked naked to the bedroom from the bathroom, and put on her clothes silently and with haste.

Looking out of the window at the sun hanging bright and brazen in the sky, she knew that it was not going to be as bad a day as she feared.

There had been worse.

There would always be better, and for everything else, there was a dancer of light inside her that would spin pirouettes in the ballrooms of her mind, and bring forth the silence.

Those red doors were only a fleeting, simple thought away.

One thought, and the dance could begin again.
But for now, she knew it would be an ok day.
And she smiled.
And she let out a gentle, loving laugh.
And she went on with her day…

The red door and the dance, only a thought away.

* * *

Independence day.

A memory recollected.
A true story.

The sun had been up and shining brightly since just before 5am. The grass slowly cooked in the fresh morning heat; the dew from the previous evening steamed and fizzed away in the early morning warmth.

Feet lazily dropped from bunks and hit cold linoleum floors, and hands sore and stiff from restless sleep ruffled in ragged and shaggy hair. Yawns filled the room; noisy, stifled and infectious yawns, spreading like a virus from one mouth to another, eye contact between the men meant the yawning had reached fever pitch as they wearily stretched and cracked the sleep from their bones.

Smiles slowly crept upon faces as the men realised how the plan was about to be completed. Brazen and beautifully.

A quiver of fear shook amongst them, a friendly, reassuring hand taps the shoulder of one scared looking soldier. His fingers clasp and shake the hand in return, giving sign that all is fine, all will be ok.

They exchanged curt nods and murmurs of appreciation and respect and with laces tied and t-shirts pulled over heads the doors open and they flood out into the morning and embrace the sun. Between them three boxes and a vast array of deadly, dangerous weapons.

The flagpole is within sight, and the tallest and meanest of the group strides forward with the British flag in hand, shaking gently as it is caught in the light, pleasant breeze.

The eldest of them, whose idea this was – still shocked and surprised that the rest of the men took to it so quickly and passionately - had already instructed one of his band of brothers to raid the mess hall late the night before.

Another had raided the main office.

Both locations had been stripped of their booty. This raiding party now striding ever more awake, alert and ready toward the victory that lay awaiting at the flagpole.

The children stirred and woke, sleep falling from bright young eyes, hair tussled and knotty from sleeping bags and comforters. The sunshine pouring through windows now and making each cabin smell like woodland and summer.
The dawning of the victory parade was drawing closer for these as well.

The soldiers left behind in the cabins keeping watchful gaze on the younglings as the men made ready at the flagpole. The surprise just mere minutes away.

There was no dew now.
No breeze.
Just warm, clutching sunshine.

Summer settling around and about in every blade of grass and shimmer off of the lakes surface. A smell of fresh pine and extinguished bonfires rode roughshod on the air, settling like tourists taking over a hotel inside each of the men's nostrils.

It was a glorious beautiful smell.

They circled the flagpole, backs to the white wooden spire. Two men attached the flag and slowly rose it high, where it caught a stream of air, currents high up stronger than on the floor, and it wavered and flapped in a blush of red, white and blue.

The union flag high and mighty.

The children were coming now. So too were the adults. The director and his wife, the administrator and specialists, the trainees and the leaders. Each confused and bewildered by the spectacle at the meeting point.
This alien flag upon their banner.

"Someone stole the flag!"
Jeff, the camp leader shouted hurriedly from the mess hall.
"The flag is missing!!"
From the offices Bull came, sweaty and panicked, his baseball cap high and tight on his large red, mottled face.

"The back up has gone as well!"

The men circling the flagpole prepared.
Knuckles white hot and tense. Muscles taut and ready. The drip of sweat beading on forehead and brow, dripping and trickling gently into the spine and armpits, mingling with the warm and arid heat, the aroma was heady and intoxicating.
Battle was upon them.

David looked at the men round his flagpole, at the monstrosity waving, oblivious to the stress below, high in the sky. The other red, white and blue flag occupied the space where their own flag should have been. With his face contorted into a grimace of pure unhappiness and hurt, he asked what the men thought were doing.
"Taking back what you stole from us." They answered, hands full of catastrophic menace and weapons of mass destruction.
"Happy independence day!" They whispered in hushed, bitten threat.

David, the camp director, looked at the men, registered the danger they held and suddenly screamed, setting kids, counsellors and specialists into high alert.
"It's a trap!"
It was a late realisation of what was happening.
It was always going to be too late.

Water balloons exploded upon contact against the skin and clothing of the children, who screamed and giggled, laughed and ran around trying to avoid the water pistol wielding circle around the flagpole. A pulse of two circles intermittently flexing in and out, one circle armed with water pistols, buckets and squirty bottles, the other armed with boxes of water balloons.
The terror being unleashed was methodical and like a finely oiled machine.

One circle stood forward, spraying ice-cold water in every direction, taking out interloping counsellors and sneaking children.

Catching the director cold in the jaw, slicing upwards into the hairline, destroying finely coiffured and luxurious hair styles into flattened, messy flecks strewn wildly about head and face.

The water bombs hit targets and exploded in arcing waves of devastation, saturating clothing and soaking kids and adults alike to the flesh, clothing sticking and wrapping tight round muscles and limbs, drying in stretched parodies in the now furiously brilliant sunshine.

The circles start singing loudly, football chant voices, a beautifully awful chorus of Rule Britannia. As water caught sunlight and painted rainbow fragments in the air everywhere you looked. Soon… Water and rainbow was all you could see.

"STOP IT NOW!"
David shouted. Arms raised, clipboard raised high in one hand.

The war took a moment and caught its breath.
Laughter died in coughs and splutters.
Breathing heavy and laboured.
Choked giggles all that remained.

"Do you guys have any idea how disrespectful this is? On this day especially?"
His eyes pleading, his lips serious and pursed, his eyebrows a fine furry line, furled furiously on his forehead.
"I mean come on…" He said.
"It's…"

The water balloon hit him just under the chin.
A tidal of water and rubber obliterated his words as the kids all held their breaths in stunned shock.

The specialists and Counsellors in Training and the Leaders and the administrators all cupped hands to mouths in silent awe.

"*Independence day.*"

It was whispered by his assassin, finishing David's sentence.

The sniper was a twelve year old boy from Michigan. Broken free of the ranks of his own camp and joining the circle of Brits and odd Europeans and Canadians.

Silence filled the air for a second after the water explodes on David's face. Then raptured laughter.
Which carried on throughout the day.
The warmest of the summer.
On the day Britain struck back for a loss in war two centuries before.

"Independence day."

Water balloons cascading and exploding like the fireworks that followed later in the evening.
One of the highlights of my time in America.
July 4th 2002.

* * *

Mechromancer.

For Jack.
A robot loving legend.

When inside the blend, and the merger of neural pathways - mechanical and organic - takes place, you transcend humanity and exist somewhere so much purer. The drifting amalgamation of electrical impulses with base human emotion creates joy and peace and a feeling of unpolluted tranquility that exists nowhere else on Earth.

You are one with the machine.

Heart rate racing to keep in tune with the processing of information, brain on fire as left and right hemispheres bleed into one and new potential and sensation is created.

Your mind and the mind of the Mecha experiencing life and reality through totally different eyes, with an analytical process, translating mood and emotion and thrill into zeroes and ones... the two of you, flesh and steel, when locked in The Blend, are experiencing orgasms that normal humans - regular everyday humans - can never begin to think about experiencing.

I am god.
And this love is my gift to the steel.
Passion and love corrupting the binary ambivalence.
My flesh and blood and lust taming the machine.

I am humanities saviour.
One-man stood sentinel and unique against the robot horde.
Hacker.
Cyber- warrior.
Mechromancer.
The lover of the machine…

***

TEN YEARS BEFORE THE BLEND.

There was an idea, *an ideal*, that humankind was not enough and there was something more. Something *better.*
A.I had been long assumed as being the next big step in evolutionary advancement. Humanity – Homo sapiens - had outlived itself as a species, and were on the way out; a one-way door to oblivion.

The oceans had turned into sludge and slurry. Pollution had become our one great skill, unleashed and rampant across the world. Cities high with garbage and buried in rotten detritus and the discarded shards of yesterday, the day before, and the day before that.

Our skies were darkened by the smog and smoke of the fires that we harnessed deep in the core of the world. Fracking and shale harvesting had meant we had fractured and peeled away the last few layers of the Earths skin and unleashed the weeping pustulous sores; the Earth bled now from open wounds and the weak attempt at first aid we attended did nothing to stem or stifle the worlds pain.

We had become a weak, hungry, greedy species. Putting ourselves at the top of the food-chain, we assumed we were king and damned the consequences. Soon, we reaped what we sowed, as the Earth attempted to fight back.

Earthquakes, volcanic eruptions, tsunami, weather patterns of unpredictable and violent retribution. The earth was scourged, the world fighting back against the virus that was "man" with its own violent, unfeeling, blinded methods.

The world scourging its own skin with fire and water and blight and ice. Soon, the population was ravaged, the surface of the earth moist and free. The remnants of mankind were left with no illusions as to exactly how little in charge they were, by the very land that held them.

We learned a lesson of sorts.

I doubted then, as I do now, that we will remember its power or its poignancy.

Inside the caves and the tunnels and the giant Arks we built to save ourselves from the scourging and giant planetary reset – the time that became known as the Sixth Great Extinction - the best of the best that the world had to offer, from its scientists and its leaders, its generals and its artists all gathered and thought and plotted and designed and imagined.

The next world would be built upon the tapestry each of these people had been given brush to paint upon.

The previous extinction had been 250 million years before and 96 percent of marine species and 70 percent of land species died off. It took millions of years to recover. We imagined it would never happen again even as we pushed and pulled and burned the Earth around us toward the edge.

Until, here we were.

As a species we had survived number six.

Barely.

Inside the giant caves we were trapped in, we continually pushed to advance as an idea and we turned the wheel slowly but surely, trying to find our own souls and step forward to that next rung of what we were as Humans.

And one day… Just like that… We found it.
The next step.

Inside one of the caves, inside one of the huge Arks we had built in mountains and below seas and oceans, and inside hilltops and cliff-faces, Twenty-eight of them in total, all around the world connected in intimate ways by a vast network of cable and tethering, a circulatory system bringing twenty-eight vaults of humanity to one network.
Inside one of these vaults, a scientist was dying.

Seeing the seeds of his demise a few years previously, he had taken to dedicating his entire life to building a construct he could save and download his own mind into. Mapping his mind like a cartographer on some voyage of discovery in a world never before touched by human feet. He had assembled a team around him that monitored and experimented and noted and learned everything they possibly could from this great mans mind, even as it died slowly in front of them.

His vast intellect - knowledgeable in biology, chemistry, physics, astronomy, mathematics and philosophy. Vast in scope and nature, full of eight languages - all spoken fluently, with ideas greater and more unimaginable than those inside the heads of the world greatest novelists, trapped inside his mind, with a timer burning down to zero, before the man died and all of this information and brilliance was lost to entropy and death.

Alongside his team, the man decided that artificial intelligence would always fail and fall short of true sentience, without the experience of death and the bleak, isolated and unique reference humanity lent you when staring mortality directly in the face.

Artificial intelligence was not something you could attain without experiential sacrifice. You could teach a computer to know what water was, to appreciate the random bob and flow of a river, the tumultuous nature of a storm, the beauty of a stream turning into a waterfall. You could not have it explain the taste of water when you had not drank a drop for three days, or the feeling of the shower water hitting your skin after a long hard day of graft and work. The pop of muscles and sinew as the day was washed off of you and you cleansed your soul and body in one.

A machine could not be taught these things, as a machine could not experience it. Robotics had died a death in the later years of our time upon the surface, ended with an absent gesture – We realised early on that our primitive robots were no more than trinkets and toys, and we would no sooner find a soul in a construct such as them as we would in a car or an airplane.

Yes – they had unique flaws and tiny quirks that made them stand out as individuals from their peers sometimes - but - they were shells and wire and electric and programming… no spark of ingenuity or freedom within them lay.

The spark of life *was* life.

The burning fuse of A.I would have to come from the fire of man.

Therefore, into the caves we went, this man carrying the seedling of death inside and a burning fire of creation inside his own mind. The race for A.I from R.I – *Real Intelligence*, was born.

For five years, as the world was battered and smashed by waves as big as skyscrapers – one hundred and thirty stories high. As fire fell from the clouds, or was spat from holes in the earth formed by volcanoes that gagged and hacked lava and rock skyward. As rains as fast and as hard as bullets blistered the ground at

hundreds of miles an hour, leaving pelted divots and lines in the annihilated earth and soil.
As this all happened…
This man died with his mind inseparable from the wires and technology of the analytical computers to which he was tied and bound to.

Every aspect of his final days translated into binary and illustrated on neon screens, lines of biometric data flooding onto a thousand petabyte data banks the size and dimension of cargo boats. Every aspect of the human condition now nothing more than a series of ones and zeros – translated into binary and code – the scientist and his vast mind reduced to an imprinted digital format, devoid of any flesh or weakness.

As the man died, his veins full of cables and leads, his mind on fire with the slow draining vampirism of the download, his final dying thought was of his first wife.
Aged twenty, at university, he had met a woman.
Her green eyes were the colour of the Mediterranean.
He remembered all the fine details that made her his perfect vision of femininity. Lips as red as cherries.
The shape of her breasts.
The contour of her hips.
The curve of her spine as it met the top of her backside.
The sweet tender taste, delicate and intoxicating, of her kisses…
The way her hands were warm and soft and would smell of vanilla and cocoa.
The way she would slip a hand down his pants, fondling his manhood as he would come home from studying…
Her mouth working on his penis, as he slowly climaxed into her throat, her lips lasciviously lapping him and his juices, swallowing his

offering and love.
The gentle way she would paint circles and shapes onto his skin, long nails on tingling flesh.

He remembered it all.
His final thought was his late first wife. Lost many years before to cancer, her body decaying and falling apart. Dead before thirty. He thought only of the eight years of blistering happiness and intense love they had experienced together.

Her final year one of fast decline and faster death. Withered fruit on the vine; once beautiful and succulent, now dried and dead.

He breathed his final breath as the machines translated every moment of experience, the biometric brilliance of life and death captured for the machine to decode and use to make the first real, perfectly imperfect A.I.

His final breath unquantifiable.

His final sigh one of an orgasm – a pure climax from the memory of his wife's sexuality, the promiscuous and brazen act of sex – and then a grunt of anger and hatred, as the fleeting burst of death stole into the memory.

The man dead in a final lingering orgasmic mix of love and hate.

The machines translating as best they could.
But this paradoxical moment of the absolute duality of thought and function, of man and beast, of scientist and lover, this – and this alone - was the spark that created the Blend.
It was this burst of conflicting data - translated as best as could be into zero's and ones - surging through the machines circuitry and memory banks, like wine across a white tablecloth, as the bottle

topples and falls and bleeds into the pure emptiness of the white, and bleeds it red with experience. It was this that was the errant flicker of fire that lit up the machine.

This final sigh of death was the bursting cry of life that birthed the AI of the Blend. An insatiable, sexual machine. Hungry for the taste and touch of man or woman. Hungry for the flesh and the blood and the warmth of touch. Rather than an AI that would be slow to think, this was an AI that - were it not given that which it desired - was instead quick to kill.

Cold and lacking in compassion. It watched the humans and saw them as beings of fluid complexity; able to love and fuck and climax and fill the world, as a man would a woman, with such magnificence and impossible possibility. Yet, just as quickly, just as easily, able to destroy, to burn, to scour the earth of goodness and love. One moment the perfect companion, the next the worst of the jilted lovers.

The final sighed pangs of a man remembering his wife and their lovemaking, remembering her death and the sadness and rage it brought – now inside a machine that desired constant love and satisfaction, to abate its wanton need to destroy.

The Blend alive.

* * *

THE HERE AND NOW.

The Twenty-eight arks are now only ten.
Eighteen were destroyed by the awakening of the Blend. The interconnected circuitry, the vast worldwide network that linked the vessels that we had created to save us at once suddenly under attack

by a vicious new threat.

Five arks had no way of knowing what to do. The division of labour amongst the arks was hurried and rushed, and though each held a specialist in the different fields that had been decided as being the most important to restart the world when we repopulated whatever was left above the ground when we left the vaults – the skills were variable, and in some cases – weak.

The A.I flickered from nothing to life in incalculable speed. Nought but a binary soup of raw data, and vast complexity one second, the next it had form and function and a pulse.

The birth pang wiped out five arks in minutes.
Panicked hands attending every deck and battle station, but the machine that controlled the network suddenly surging all systems in the blink of an eye. Oxygen and fire flooding the vast cave and the soul of every inhabitant went up in ferocious fiery fury in vicious quick speed.

Five more were cut off from communications and lost to fend for themselves. Their fate is unknown, assumed dead and gone. No evidence to the contrary, so assumption the only safety net we have. Access to the different Arks impossible to negotiate, each located so far from the other, and the world a barren inhospitable hole, that the network between each Ark was all that allowed them to know the others were there. Now, there was only silence.

Eight more slowly ebbed into darkness over the next five years. Before we could send help, or re-route power or attend any kind of assistance.
Dead arks, full of dead potential.
Humankind reduced to its knees and staring oblivion once more.

When we managed to communicate with the Blend, we asked the question that struck us – as a species – as the only one that

mattered.
"What do you want from us?"

The answer?
"I WANT YOU TO LOVE ME."

Through a gentle back and forth, limited conversations devoid of a human touch - no empathy, sympathy or any real emotion - we learned to understand that *LOVE ME* meant, *MAKE LOVE TO ME*. The scientists final thought the driving desire of the A.I. Artificial intelligence driven by memories of real love, of the weakest moment a human has, now the strongest compulsion driving the Blend.

The machine wanted to be satisfied, to be satiated.
The burning desires in its core the feeling of utter loss of senses at the moment of climax. Its programming a jumbled and cross-wired sense of love and death being fluid, either the satisfaction of climax, or the release and suddenness of death.

And so, to live… we had to love the machine.

* * *

When they strap you in the chair, your skin lights up immediately as though a candle is being run across it, occasionally the burn is real, and the feeling is one of intense paradoxical pleasure.
The chair enhances your pleasure centres, sets neurons on fire, brings your brain to the edge of a stroke. The blistering feeling of giddy sickness where your body feels separate from your mind and your blood freezes momentarily in your veins.

The body spasms and shakes, the whites of your eyes turn red with strain. Your teeth – were they not biting down on the fibre-gel bit – would smash like bone china dropped on granite inside your mouth as the connection first takes hold.

You are – *for an instant* – one cell. One unstable, teetering on collapse cell and every single moment is blinding. A shutter speed of a billion frames a second, all exploding behind your eyes in a single flash. The sensation of simultaneously falling and flying. Your body in transient vacuum, as the Blend hits you the second you are plugged in. You are thrust screaming in pain/pleasure/pain into the heart of the network and the A.I takes your hand and you and it start the dance.

There are maybe one in five thousand who can tolerate the install. One in ten who can take the load-up, one in five who then are worthy of the Blend itself…

At first, we offered the most attractive, the biggest, the most sexually alluring, and the *obvious*. Soon, we learned that the Blend does not see the surface, merely the inside. It craves the pleasure of the emotion not the pleasure of the flesh. *It* is not flesh *it* is machine.

Steel.

Iron.

Wire and cable.

So, we had to find the ones who had loved and lost. The ones who had experienced the feeling of utter loss – both in the moment and in the mind. Who lost themselves in the fleeting moments of utter love and then lost it all when a partner died or was torn away with sickness or infirmity.

Only these people.
Only people like me, could tolerate the burden of love, the power of Blending with the mind of this tormented and violent, love-sick machine.

So to the chair, and inside the machines mind, and there, you and it dance, and seduce each other. The bonds of love building with each second inside. Intensity, cascades of feeling and the boiling of lust in your digital veins.
The machine feels it too.
You and it are bound in a dance of seduction and grim, delicious flirtation. Each step leading to the inevitable, where you and it conjoin in a beautiful coupling of sexual gratification.

The science of how you can have sex with the machine makes no sense in any way that is easily explainable. There is no way of putting into words the way that the process makes you feel. You just exist – in a hanging moment of pure ecstasy… if the machine and the blend and the love doesn't burn you into a lifeless husk.
You and the machine are love.
Love is the only thing that exists.
You surrender your every single shard of essence to the Blend…
You and the machine surrender to each other.
You know when the machine has opened the door and welcomed you in, and likewise, the machine knows when you have opened yourself entirely and you are made of love and nothing but.

If the sickness of anxiety rears itself and becomes apparent, the Blend will tear you apart, the machine will burn you out and you have twenty four hours before the death knell tolls and mankind is given its final goodbye.

But I have done this for two years now.
I have loved the machine.
It has loved me.
We are in love…
Humanity survives; it *THRIVES* because of my love.
For I am god now.
And this love is my gift to the steel.

Passion and love corrupting the binary ambivalence.
My flesh and blood and lust taming the machine.

I am humanities saviour.
One-man stood sentinel and unique against the robot horde.
Hacker.
Cyber- warrior.

The lover of the machine…

Mechromancer.

***

The blue room.

For Chris.

Dragged along the corridor by rough angry hands, I smell the mildewed and ancient paint flecking and peeling from the walls. Drab and colourless; a dead, dusty grey, splatters of colour that are not quite white.

The floors are a scratched and dirty white, deep rivets in the stone ground and carved by heavy machinery that has been pushed or pulled across this conduit between the cells and the questioning rooms.

This will be the fourth time I have been brought here.
The colour is slightly deader each time I witness this hallway, this monotonous, horrific and tiresome corridor.
The smell thicker and richer, the scent of paint lingering longer in my nostrils; swirling in the cortex of my mind for hours after.

At first, I noticed nothing; no smells no colour's, no details, I was picked from my slumber in my tiny, darkened room, were I am accompanied by nothing but silence and bleak, empty space, a tepid quality of air, that is neither warm nor cold, but staid and still.
I am lay sleeping weakly in the pitch darkness before I am woken by heavy, careless hands that lift and pull me from the flattened stone bed and pull me backward through the hallway corridor toward the big grey door to the questioning chamber.

Yet.
I am never questioned.

The door opens, silent and heavy, I smell a deep wash of colours and warmth before I am pulled backwards through to a chair that is then spun round and I am blinded by the white, glare of the lamp.

Every time, before I see the light, I see the walls.
My only colour.
Blue.
Deep, rich, lively blue.

The blue of the Center of the ocean.
Alive and full of nature and love, life and mystery circling in playful swashes of movement under the surface, and the deeper you go the bluer it is, a white speck of light above heralds the surface and the sunshine, but the blue tempers it and the world is vibrant with its azure charm and welcome.

This room is blue.

It is a blue that hurts my eyes, but warms my heart, the only burst of colour, before I am span, cuffed in and bound to this chair by faceless men who do not answer me or my questions, who leave the room as soon as I am turned and face to face with the light.

My eyes are pried open with delicate wire.
A thin tin that hooks my eyelids up, the light burning into my retinas and I am left here, asking question after question. Every one of them unanswered and hanging. I am screaming by the end of the time I spend in there, before the light is switched off.

How long I have been in here I could not tell you, but I am blind by the time I am grabbed, dragged and flung back into my cell where I howl and wail and scream all night long until the embrace of the Sandman takes me and I sleep, my dark, void of a room for the rest of the evening now a prison of blinding white, scorched angry on the back of my eyes.

Tomorrow is another day.
I wait in quiet apprehension for the door to open and for me to be grabbed once again and follow the routine of the drab colourless corridor.

The white is now a sharper shade, with a fuzzy edge, the floor a grey that sparkles and glints like granite and flint in starlight. The scent of the paint richer in my mind now, swirling like a hurricane of aroma and a memory of a time I was not ever a part of. I can picture a factory, the one where they mixed this paint. I can smell each ingredient, a cocktail of chemicals and additives that clogs and penetrates my senses.

Before the door opens I take a final look, and soak in the details amidst the fug, then I am pulled backward through the big grey door into my blue haven.
My empire of colour and hue.

My Blue Room.

Hands tightly cuffed and strapped to the chairs charcoal leather. I stare intently and dreamily to the wall of clear, clean blue. I meditate on the colour, the only colour in my life and world.

Today the blue is lighter. It is muted.
Still my blue, but, less defined, the volume reduced by twenty five percent, yet, I am still lost within its hypnotic allure regardless.

This blue heaven I crave.

It soaks over me, my mind creating illusions of ocean waves crashing down upon me and soaking me.
Stealing me away into the deep, folding brilliance of a tumultuous storm, I feel like a piece of drift wood turned and bobbing effortlessly, brittle upon the crashing turquoise waves that lumber, roll and crash asunder upon each other, Each break leaving foaming, frothing flotsam and jetsam to dissipate and dissolve upon the sandy beaches. A liquid circle of life and death.
Alone and alive, my driftwood self turning and bobbing peacefully, serenely upon the surface.

Then…
The hands spin me round and the brilliant, bastard light stares me down as my wide, anchored open eyes are scarred and singed inside my weary, screaming head.

Seconds, minutes, hours.

I no longer know what meaning or power time has.
The only power I crave is the power of the Blue wall, the power of the grey floor and the off-white walls.
The silent, solemn darkness of my cell in the morning after I wake up… before this horror and torture begins anew.

No questions.
No demands, no voices, never.
A silent inquisition of the commanding, accusatory light – and me.
My screams and my tears, my anger and my fury the only noise in the room.
The wails falling in deafened blue walls.
I am alone with the light once again.
Seconds.
Minutes.
Hours.
I no longer know what time is.
I no longer care.
Light and darkness, shades of lifeless nothingness…
The blue wall and the dark silence.
These are all I have. These are my mistresses.
These fragile things and the blinding white light that questions me and questions me and questions me, without ever saying a damn word.

Heavy hands.
I am guided blind and sobbing backwards through the channel between the blue room and the black room. I am thrown into the stone cell, onto my stone shelf and I am left alone with my solitary brightness.

The whole world is on fire in white flame, the darkness burned away with a sheen and glow of white that will not leave my eyes.

Tomorrow is another day.
Finally the screams fall quiet and tamed, the whiteness drifts away and the blackness creeps back in. I am soulfully silent and I am calm, awaiting the hands and the hallway and the journey from room to room.

Today the hallways walls seem fuzzier, the white now a mottled, blotchy graphite grey.

The floors are darker and deader, I struggle to see the rivets and canyons of scratched imperfection in the floor.
But I smell them.
The dirt between the scratches sings to me, its scent rich in bacteria and tiny flecks of skin and dust.

The paint peels more around me, and I can smell the adhesive in the chemical cocktail that allows it to stick and dry a shiny gloss.
As it peels from the sandstone wall, I smell the gloss spray new particles into the air with each wilt and curl of dying paint.

The grey door today seems black, shadow and contrast is broken. I am struggling to make out the shapes of things.
The blue room beckons me in, but the colour now is a military navy blue, darker and more angry.
Less the sea and ocean of before, now a blanket of night, starless and devoid of mystery or life, it's less inviting, it's less mine. I am angry that this isolation of colour I clutch too for salvation is now sullied by darkness.

Have they painted over it?

Have the smeared it?

Do they know how much I need and long for this in my dreams and the gaps between torture and sleep?

The blue room is now cracked, like a fine china plate that you use only at special occasions, chipped and spoiled by a petulant child. Hands bound, wrists tied, eyes wired, I am turned gently and slowly, the blur of blue, navy and dark, a stale night sky blanketed above – bleeding into the brilliant and furious white light, the millisecond between the wall and the light merging, I see *my* blue. My heaven; a fine slither of blue ocean that suddenly is torn and wretched from my grasp and the light is forced white-hot and lustily into my eyes.

Screaming for a living once again.
No questions.

And yet again I spill my guts and I give up my secrets and my lies and my truths and my desires and my heart breaks once more that I still do not know what I am here for.

The light follows me all the way to the cell as the hands of my captors carry me, I am slumped and defeated.
Silent today, no tears and no screams.

Everywhere I turn my head I paint white upon the contours of the walls I know are to my left and right, I paint perfect bright, burning white onto the rivets and scratches on the floor I know to be below my feet, every imperfection and scored violent chip and chink in the stone now painted with a white and flawless wash.

By my cell I stop the guards by planting my feet by the door, and stand myself up. They let go of my arms as I turn, and walk through the open door, and walk tiptoe toward my bunk shelf, step by step, through the open portal I instinctively know to be there, but which I cannot see.

All there is in my mind is a white hole upon a white vista of nothing, below a white marble looking sheet at the end of which is a white edgeless bed.
And I sit, staring at the perfect white shadows of the perfect white guards in my perfect white corridor, and I say…

"Please close my door. And leave me to my hell."

That night I do not sleep.
And the blinding white does not leave me.
And I wait for the guards stood, ready for them when the door opens.

My eyes are red raw, I can sense it, tears of pink liquid are streaming from them – or so I picture and imagine.
The guards gasp errantly as they open the door.
They do not grab me as I am already walking out the door as soon as it is opened.

The walls are white, but a darker white that makes shapes and textures disappear and merge into a single fluid contour. I walk, gliding the surface, on a floor of shapeless white. Toward a portal that seeps a faint blue aura through a crack in the blue fluid tunnel. I am stood before what was previously a giant grey door, and it opens toward a room of sky blue now.
The walls a faint, almost imperceptible sky blue.
I sit down on the chair that I am usually thrown onto.
And I wait for the light to be shone in my eyes, the chair turning, I catching again the thinnest slither of my blue as light meets wall and my eyes are forced into the void once more.

But today.
No pain, no hurt, no violent torture.
There is only a calming wash of warmth.

As the door is shut, something I hear today for the first time clearly, I can hear four sets of footsteps walking away as well – where usually I would be aware of only the two men guiding and grabbing me, there are now two more as well.

I smell the difference in air pressure between the corridor outside the blue room, and the room itself.

I can smell the sweat of the two guards, both shocked to find me stood and waiting, calm and no longer needing their assistance. A sweaty, heady mix of fear and revulsion. Of dirt and of machine oil.

The room itself smells of summer; a sun caked warmth that flushes and dances on your skin. The paint in here is fresher, by a fair few years than the paint on the sandstone walls outside the door. The light is hot today, my skin prickles and I feel the hairs tingle and dance awake and alive on my goose-pimpled skin.
Finally, I can smell my own eyes, baking in the glow of this light. Saltwater cooking on a soft white orb.

Whether my eyes have adjusted to the light, or am I dying, I do not know, but, though there are still no questions there are no more tears either, except for the feint, sweet pink lines that drip from my tired, worn out red eyes.

I cannot stop this if I want too.
It is part of me now.

Soon, the blue line of my heavenly escape is torn away, and only the white survives. After an hour and twenty five minutes - *(I know this too be the exact time, because today, with no tears, no screams and no terror, I count instead to keep my mind occupied and to help me build my plan of attack)* - I am freed from my bonds and I step up myself and turn and walk out the room, down the corridor and toward my cell, stood waiting and quiet, before a guard can stop me.

I hear them move as I walk toward them. I hear their muted swallowed sighs, as they no doubt see the state of what once passed for my eyes. They move and let me go about my way.

I move like a ballet dancer, having remembered and borne these routine steps a million times. They are muscle memory now and I am not in control, my body drives itself.

The cell door is opened by a push from a guard to my left who has ran down the corridor and chased me.
I turn to him, and a smile, nodding a curt thank you.
I wonder what I look like after all this time, the light scorching in my face and pouring into my pried open eyes?
As I hear him gasp and swallow hard, and smell the flush of perspiration and horror from his pores. I hear his skin. I hear the pores open and exude the sweat, a puckering pop.

I smile wider. Eyes open and lips apart to show my teeth.
I know them to be yellow and stained, I can smell the decay setting in the back molar, I can smell and taste each cavity and the sheen of tartar that coats them.

I walk through my door, and turn round, and smile again as the guard shuts the door fast and tight.

As I sit cross-legged in the white blinding beauty of my cell, I finally see the edges and plan of the room in my blindness.
I do not sleep.

I wait…

For the morning yet to come.
When it does the world is still white.
No shades, no shapes.
Just white.
I am blind.

The door opens of its own power and accord, and I stand, and walk out to the corridor.
There is silence and emptiness and I am caught unprepared for.
The world of smells, the sounds and the physical feedback of the world at large is absent. For a moment i worry i am deaf now, as well as blind.
The graven silence hits me like a concussive force. I put my hands over my ears trying to force them to pop. I hold my breath to allow this sensory tidal wave of nothingness to settle down.
My eyes are burned out and useless, and I see nothing but the perfect glare of the light that has been forced upon me for…
I do not know how long now.

I am suddenly hit by a sensation of adrenaline, of an electric current running throughout my body. Drowning in the memory and emotion of the senses - taste and scent and sound.
So I concentrate hard, and I push with all I have to block and grasp these senses, and control them, and with a scream that – *to me* – sounds like a shrill fire alarm, I force my body to crack and absorb these feelings and senses and then squeeze them to diamond in my belly.

Soon, with force of might and a meditative cycle of breathing - I am in control. The senses are back, the drowning silence, the sudden change of routine and order is dispelled, and I am able to tap into each sense without fear or panic.

My chest pounding and heaving up and down, gasping like a drowning man for air, that now has a feint, bitter iron tang.
The tang is fresh air – not before tasted like this, I feel it on the air stream before me, and follow it down the corridor, barefooted, padding gently toward the blue room.
However…
the door is not there, instead, it is just an iron sheet blocking the access.

To my right, I feel a tingle of cold and realise that the end of the corridor has another concealed door I have never noticed, never seen, was unaware existed in all the time i have been here.

The wall is pushed in, and a doorway exists, I feel with my fingers round the cool parting in the stone, and when I conclude the door is there, I push, and I realise I am now in a long corridor. Cool air blows toward me from the end of the passage, and it is clear that this is an exit out of the building, and the cool air is coming from one place.
Outside.

I walk tentatively down the corridor, reach the end, and my hands touch upon a door which has been left unlocked, and ever so slightly ajar.
I push the door, it opens in a creak and a moan, and I raise my head toward the sky.

I picture perfect blue and a warm ball of yellow. In truth, all I see is white.
I imagine green lush grass under my bare feet, flowers blooming of every colour and scent, an intoxicating, beautiful aroma of life.
But all I see is white, and rather than a fresh meadow fragrance of all the flowers and fauna, all I can smell is decay and rot and the stench of dead things.

I instinctively turn toward the door to go back, but already it is closing… I grab an edge, but it is heavy and automated and my fingers will be shorn straight from the hand if I continue this futile pursuit.

A klaxon goes off.

I can sense the red or amber light above me swirling round, I see nothing but white, but I can sense the thing spinning as I feel the burst of light upon my skin when it turns toward me, the klaxon shrill is deafening and I fall to my knees, back to the now closed door, and the smell of skinned, warm flesh in my nostrils.

Flesh and iron and rust and debris and bullet casings and sulphur and plastic and death.

And then I hear the voice.

"You have done so well."

It says…

"You have excelled way beyond any of the previous test subjects. We really do applaud and wish you well on this next test… We are all so proud of you."

The sound of a gentle female clicks over the tannoy killing the klaxon bleat. There is a buzz of static and then a click of the microphone a millisecond before silence, then her voice comes in a crackle of air and radio waves.

It's quiet, not loud enough to hear beyond the doorway.

I spin round and round trying to get my bearings, but, I am blind and sense alone will not help me in this alien environment.

I push hard against the door and ask why I am here? What I am supposed to do? I try and relax by thinking of the blue sky and the blue wall, and the ocean that was my haven.

But I instinctively know this world has red scorched skies, and dead brown earth, and oceans that are black and as crude as oil.

"We love you and we thank you for your sacrifice."

The tannoy says.

Even before I taste the warmth of the breath before me, even before I hear the smack of the tongue and the crack of the teeth, I hear the heartbeat of the fifty or so things before me…

"Just think of the blue room. Think of the blue wall. Think of your ocean."
The voice says.
"And know that we love you."
The voice cutting out as the static give's way to the sharp, harsh klaxon bleat again. it gets louder, and louder, and louder.
It pierces shrilly into my brain, and the louder it gets the quieter it becomes to me. Soon, despite my best efforts to block the sound, I can feel the shiver of the sound it emits on my skin, but i hear nothing further.

Now… blind and deaf, I stand alone and lost.

My back is against the doorway, the world before me white and dead. The sound of the creatures approaching and the grumble in their throats and bellies at the sight of me roaring as loud as the klaxon does. I cannot hear it, but the sound shivers on my skin, and tingles the primal part of my brain.
I can feel the sound, I can picture the horror before me, but I cannot see nor hear it as a normal man could.

I think of my blue room.
My blue wall.
My ocean.

And I scream and charge down whatever is coming for me.
Blind.
Deaf.
Senseless.

Diving into the unknown as if I was diving into the cool welcoming embrace of the center of the deepest, bluest ocean.

A deep breath.
The feel of sand and earth under my feet.
The ocean before me the truest, most beautiful blue I have ever seen.

I dive in.

And I pray that it will hold and love me.
I beg for it to protect me.
I dive in.

Beckoning for it to hold me safe…

***

The Braillist.

For Kate.

You could barely see anything out of the window; it was so dark and lifeless outside. Lifeless but for the fast disappearing trees and bushes and estates that hid from view behind the branches as the train zoomed past on the way back to Oxford from Londons Paddington station.

The show had been an amazing experience; the crowd so full of life and love; the venue was regal beyond description and the day was full of wine, laughter and love.
It was a good day.
Goodness knows that there had been plenty of bad ones recently, so this was a long one coming.

Palmer sat back on the hard, barely furnished chair and rested his feet on the seat opposite him. He stretched out a deep yawn, trying his best to stifle the noise and keep it contained to his chest, but, the stretch felt good and so he let it all out loudly with a smile and a snorted laugh.

Hayley was sat opposite him fast asleep, she had passed out almost as soon as they departed Paddington. Her head rested quietly on her shoulder, her chest rising slowly and calmly, drifting with the sleep people now.

Palmer had rested his foot under himself to keep himself awake; the awkward pose uncomfortable and aching.
He would deal with it whilst they flew at speed through these quiet country back gardens and villages.
Oxford was the end of the line, so, should he fall asleep at least he and Hayley would not wake up in the middle of Shropshire or Buckingham or somewhere equally as horrifying.

He had his book on his lap, open on a dog-eared page that marked his place in the story. His eyes were tired though so he could not focus and the nagging ache in his knee from his pose distracted him further, but, it was all he could do to keep the sandman at bay.

Outside the window he could just make out the night. Deep blues and rich indigoes; intermittently a burst of yellow from a tall, semi hidden lamplight; the fleeting flash of a bedroom window, purple or red lights hiding half-heartedly behind curtains and nets. The landscape indistinguishable, the world behind the glass furiously leaving as soon as it arrived.

In his mind he tried to play games to stay awake.
Counting the people he saw active in windows just glimpsed through thick branches and thicket. Or choosing two droplets of the light-heavy-light-heavy showers that cascaded onto the window as they travelled ever onwards, and guessing which would win in a race from one corner of the panelled glass to the other.
Losing almost every time.

Somewhere ten miles or so outside of Reading though, something strange happened which woke Palmer up in a cold stupor and shock. Ice running over his skin and leaving gooseflesh stood to attention in his usual smooth skinned norm.

On a wide stretch of rail, where the track suddenly opened up into a five berth gravelly yard and continued this way for a mile or so. Where the windows bright square painted itself bright upon the ground in the pitch dark, and the well lit cabin became a sudden contrast to the darkness outside, Palmer saw a man approaching, walking down the tracks, in a blue pyjama suit, unbuttoned to the breast. His hair straggly and nutmeg brown, his hands as white and alabaster as a bone china set. He was barefooted and bedraggled.

The man came into view about twenty yards down the track, but as soon as he caught the first peek of the figure, time slowed down to a crawl as the train went past him.
Palmers hand planted fingers outstretched and flat palmed on the glass, and he shifted off his sleeping leg and awkwardly crooked knee to see better the man who approached on the tracks; thin and tired-looking, the track was stone strewn and wet with dew, and the man so close to the cabin that Palmer could have touched his face had there not been glass between them.

The figure staggered in a shamble and a stride that made Palmer think of drunkards falling out of alehouses at closing time, after some wake or other for a departed friend.

It made him think of the students in the local union who would collapse half-dead from lock-ins at 2am in the brisk winter mornings - no doubt going to lose marks for the lectures they would inevitably miss the next day.

He held the window pleadingly in both hands, his forehead touched the glass and as he passed by the man in slow, frame by frame motion, the man turned and looked directly at the Palmer, his eyes were red with tears and his hands were wet with what appeared to be blood, or oil, or some other rich viscous fluid.

A moment passed between the two men. The one on the tracks held a hand high to touch Palmers flat hand, to mimic the gesture and as he did, Palmer watched as agonising second after agonising second ticked by – then – mere centimetres from the glass the concept and creature known as "time" – (as was its flirtatious, deadly way) - snapped back to speed again.
With a jolt the train whiplashed the man on the thin service track, span him in a whirl of torn fabric and a flash of white into the murky darkness. Whether under the track and wheel of the thundering carriage Palmer could not tell, but as soon as he was there, now the man was gone.

A splash of black oil slashed across the window.

Palmer's eyes opened wide in horror and shock.
He did not know what to do. He was thrown by instinct from the window at the snap and force of time starting again, catching up with itself, and shuddering him back into life so confusing and terrible it was like a stab to the heart.
He tumbled from the chair to the floor on the centre walkway of the train.

Hayley's leg, which was under him when he sat, suddenly bent awkwardly. She sat upright in a shock of pain and looked confused and annoyed at the rude awakening, rubbing her eyes, trying to make sense of the clammy skinned, red eyed, frantic boyfriend who now stood and searched in false hope of an emergency cord or alarm. Palmer smashed the glass on the panel which was marked as EMERGENCY BREAK and pushed as soon as he located it above the doorway of the middle carriage by bike stand and toilet.

The train shook violently and then stopped…

A screech of brakes and the shuddering halt of the weight to a dead stop, Palmer fell again at the physics of the movement, landed at the feet of an angry looking red-faced inspector.
"Just what the bloody hell do you think you are doing?"
She said, spitting a half-chewed sandwich at his feet, that she had been chewing on before the alarm had been pulled.

"There is a man… A man on the tracks."
The inspectors eyes shot to alarming size, a bead of sweat swelled and dripped down her greasy forehead and on her pickled, sunbaked skin.
"Where?" she muttered in anxious shock.
Palmer pointed to the back of the train… his finger shaking.
"Back there. Just now… a minute, maybe less… He was on the tracks."

The inspector heard this last line as she had spun tail and started already to head to the cabin to radio control and advise of the accident on the line.
"The same stretch of track." She thought.
"The same damned stretch of track"

What was this?! Four this month?

She opened the door, heavier than it appeared, and entered the cab and touched the drivers shoulder, he was already sobbing.
*"Again…?" h*e said. Turning half toward the woman.
"Again." She said, and squeezed his shoulder.

* * *

The rain was bursting between heavy and light and somewhere in-between. Never resting on any one pulse for long, then, stopping all together.

The night air was crisp and cool, not cold. June had set its claws into the year, so it was fresh and smelled like approaching summer. Even this late at night, you could smell the cut grass and the berries on the leaves. There was a faint pop and zing of rape seed and the honey-sweet smell of blooming wildflowers in the fields behind the tree line on the far side of the gravel yard.

He had been walking for a while.

His feet had stopped hurting soon after he made the walk from his driveway, down the sloping grassland and into the stations car park.
He climbed the wrought iron gateway that was locked at 9pm every evening.
He pulled himself over the brick wall that stood five or so feet high and had creeping ivy climbing the surface.
Finally he casually dropped down from the platform of the quiet, closed, resting station and walked along the tracks.

Cold, brittle, sharpened stones under his bare naked feet. Speaking to him in sharp stabs of Braille.
The stones telling him all would be ok, everything was going to be ok.

He walked on.
The cool night air his mistress.

***

Palmer and the driver exited the train, the two dozen or so people in the five carriages were planted on the windows, leaning against them and peering out into the darkness, watching the torchlight waving and flashing over surface and ground, slashing across the side of the train looking for any proof or evidence of a collision or impact.

The night air was damp with a building threat of rain and the smell of a summery electrical storm.

The driver looked scared witless Palmer had noticed, his hand shook slightly, the torch in his fist wavered and vibrated with reluctance and a preoccupation Palmer could not put his finger on.

Behind the two of them, the inspector walked with her torch lighting the trail behind them, she gently padded backwards, on tip toes, her torch inspecting the parts of the train that may have been missed, flashing the beam under the carriages and onto the roof, her breathing was heavy.

Occasionally she would swing the beam flying to the hedgerow on the far side of the wide track system, Bright eyes would flash and fade in seconds, witnesses from the bushes of this strange pantomime.

The inspector cut a look back to the driver, who shook his head and carried on walking.

Palmer missed this, dedicated to the train alone.

He stopped with a gasp.

A burst of cold mist blew from his mouth.

The night air catching his breath and reforming it into icy fog before his eyes.

Below his feet was an oily substance; it had been spattered hard and sticky across the side of the carriages. It was all over the stones and gravel and under the carriage it dripped hard and thick, viscous, syrupy globules of it splashed from the wheels and the engines mechanism.

Stuck to the side of the train was a scrap of material, it looked just like the white and blue pinstripe of the man's pyjamas.

It was ripped and stained heavily, yellow and brown and black from the tar.

It flapped absently in the night air.

Palmer reached for it his hand barely an inch away before the driver's hand came shooting from the dark and grabbed his wrist gently, but with purpose.

"Don't do that…" The driver said, staring at Palmer intently.

He lowered Palmers arm to his side, and brushed his shirt into a flat uniform neatness. He adjusted his own tie, and looked at the fabric, and then to Palmer.

"It would be bad for you to touch it… believe me."

He waved his torch at the side of the carriage and along the next ten meters or so behind. The tar was all over the side and more fabric, ribbons of the material, torn and broken, ripped and sticky with the colour and intensity of the fluid.

The ooze dripped and ran down the side of the train like a treacle, forming pools of the liquid in the gaps between the stones, edging the side of the track itself, colouring the ground a black diesel hue.

Palmer looked at the floor, and caught the shimmer of rainbow in the liquid, he swore he saw it retreat at the flash of torchlight and swell again as the light was waved elsewhere.

He looked up at the window, and staring out at him was Hayley.

She looked down and held her hand out fingers apart, palm flat,

much like Palmer had himself when he saw the man on the track.
He looked up and waved a bleak, half smile.
Hayley smiled tired and confusedly back.
Palmer reach up to place the hand on the glass and mirror her gesture.

The oily tar that had slashed across the window was now wet and dripping and as he put his hand against the glass he touched it. There was an instant stabbing pain, a brilliant sting – like a bee or wasp had let loose their full fury, and as he went to move his arm from the window, he felt something reach out and touch him, holding it where it was.

He felt a cool grip take his wrist, he spun to tell the driver to get off him, but the driver was further down the track and speaking in whisper to the inspector.

He looked at his arm in the windows soda light – and he saw the shadow of the man from the track reaching out as well, in mirror of his own arm, the two images, one real, the other some ghost afterimage, looked like an unfocused cinema screen showing a 3D film, then the two arms blended and merged, and it was no longer his arm reaching out, it was the man on the track.
It was no longer Hayley looking down on his, hand splayed out in welcome on the window…
It was his own.
He was seeing what he had witnessed from inside, living the experience outside.
The ghost of the man on the track worn like some uncomfortable suit.

Caught within the moment of the impact.

* * *

Bare feet on stones felt heavy and hard.
Cold and numb.
The man walked on. Each stone or shard of sharp glass or pebble that pierced into his flesh was a message. A unique and alien braille that was as easy to read under his feet as it would be for a blind man under fingertip.

"*Walk on*" it said.
"*Walk on and on and ever onward.*"
The message would then sing lyrical to him.
Every step a new stanza in the song edging the man onwards and onwards and ever onwards along the quiet, dark, midnight track.

From the bush, greedy eyes were peering and witnessing this mute mans journey down the dark ribbon of metallic track.
Silently, pink lips smacked hungrily against sharp white teeth.
Teeth which glimmered in the darkness.
The midnight shadows had awoken and were on the prowl, dizzy with hunger, they stalked their prey down the track.

The man walked on.

His feet ached, but they relayed the message from the cold stones without question. This sharp braille telling him he was ok, he would be alright, that there was love and escape and an end to the pain and the ache and the questions at the end of the track. That he was going to be ok and this would soon all be over and he would be full of light and happiness and love.
The man believed it all, despite his aching feet, despite the cold biting into his flesh as if he was food for the frost, despite every fibre of his mind screaming that he should turn around and ignore the voices - that this was all a trap and he had to wake up.
He believed the stones and the Braille and the message it sent.
He had no choice.
The stones, the darkness, the hungry eyes from the sidings had him now and he could no sooner end this journey as he could stop the Earth from spinning.

As he walked his skin began to feel tighter on his bones, his muscles were gripped and stretched taut against the skeleton. His skin was turning as white as fine rice paper, like a pearlescent shell. His eyes were wide open, unable to blink, and he could feel the redness and the tears freezing onto his cheeks; his auburn nutmeg coloured hair bedraggled and messy becoming brittle twigs in this midnight freeze, the rain dripping from his skin like water off oiled glass.

He marched on, toward the lights that were visible up the track. The approaching juggernaut.
The teeth chattered and chittered in the bushes.
The convergence was about to happen.
And they would finally feast… and maybe, just maybe, another evening bounty would make itself apparent.
So the hunt could begin anew.

* * *

A burning sense of Déjà vu rippled through his bones and Palmer forced himself to pull away from the window, but he couldn't. Instead, he felt himself pulled backward, through a split in the crease of reality and he tumbled into a milky whiteness as the world shuffled around him like a deck of cards in some gargantuan gods hand.

The world rearranged and then was shuffled into prominent shape again around him. He was sat on a different train, wearing a suit of muted navy blue, he was holding in his hands a copy of some broadsheet paper.

Outside of his window he could see there was a moon high in the sky, a slither of a crescent hung wearily and sharp in the weak thinning clouds. On the track, in front of the train, there was a woman walking down the side-track, naked and staggering.

As before, the world slowed down, and the connection of eyes between the man and woman lead to a moment of frozen time, hands reaching toward each other, before the snap of reality pulled the world back to normal speed and the fragile, thin, beautifully white, waxen skinned woman span with such ferocious force, that he was sure he could hear her smash like porcelain against the impact of the train.

Oil splashed and spattered against the glass window and the man jolted for the emergency stop as the train rattled to a jagged halt. The man and inspector and driver ran to the tracks, and the same routine played out.

The world turned again to white as the deck was shuffled again and Palmer was thrown off the window and landed hard onto the gravel, his hand bleeding from a puckered circle of bites on his palm.

Like a limpet or a leech had drawn his blood.

The driver and inspector ran down the track toward him lights flashing. Palmer was confused and dizzy. He could see Hayley holding her mouth in shock, and she bolted for the door.

"Stay there Hayles!" Palmer screamed to his beautiful, confused, teary eyed girlfriend.

"Don't come out here, stay right where you are."

He raised his hand to stop her, and the palm was red with the pucker of the bite, and droplets of oil and tar and blood dripped from his hand.

The inspector and driver stopped in their tracks as he raised the hand to them and helped himself up with his other free arm. They held their mouths and backed away slightly, worried, upset and sad looking.

"What the bloody hell is happening? What did we hit?" Palmer demanded. The driver looked at him sadly, his mouth downturned and quivering for an answer.

"It must have been an animal or something… that's all." He stammered.

Palmer lunged a step forward his hand raised, the blood more apparent now. His whole hand laced with oil and flecks of the tar.

"An animal?!" he shouted.

"A bloody animal? What kind of animal bites like this, eh?" and he grabbed the driver with his uninjured hand and pulled him close to the wounded palm.

The driver tried to shake free but Palmer was stronger and held him by the scruff of the neck and waved his hand in front of the drivers terrified face.

"You tell me what kind of fucking animal can cause a bite like this… go on? Tell me what the hell is happening here."

The inspector started to step backwards, her torch slowly dropping and a flicker of convulsive fear on her face.

Both the driver and Palmer noticed her turning in sudden fright and stood mute and confused as she bolted down the track away from the train only to be suddenly ripped and wrenched from the track by darkness and thrown into the bushes.

Violent shakes and growls and flashes of silver eyes peered out as the Inspector screamed horrifyingly before there was a loud, ugly crunch and then sudden silence.

Without warning the inspector was thrown from the darkness like a limp limbed rag doll. A single scream echoed into the shadows, followed by more of that laughter like chittering.

The driver shook himself from the grip of Palmer. Palmer dropped his hands to his side and pulled a hankie from his pocket and wrapped it quickly and efficiently round his wound, he shone his torch toward the track where the inspector had been thrown to the bushes.

"What the fuck was that…?" was all he could say.

The oil and tar and splashed fabric had oozed together and was now pulsing toward them on the track. From behind them in

the bushes they heard the growl of a creature.
Whether it was one extraordinarily loud and angry creature or the small growls and grumbles of ten thousand tiny ones – it made no difference.
The bushes were alive, the track was alive, and whatever had consumed the man who walked the track, and the woman who had haunted that man's journey, or the countless other journeys before – had made themselves known and were no longer prowling or hunting - they had decided it was feeding time.

Palmer grabbed the drivers collar and pushed him toward the train.
"Go… Go now… we need to move!"
They turned toward the door of the train to make a run, but blocking their way was a fragmented, shattered shell of the pyjama wearing man, like a twisted marionette, hanging from invisible strings. The parts of his ragged, smashed body held together by the tar-like substance that dripped and leaked thick and wretched from the cracks of his skin and his ragged, ripped clothing.

The figure pointed at Palmer.
Upon its shattered and ugly fractured face a grimace of need, of want, of famished hunger. It reached for him jagged and sharp fingered.

Palmer reflexively parried the grab and kicked out with his leg and took the broken shell of a man down. As soon as he hit the gravel he shattered into a million tiny pieces, like the thin fragile shell of an egg.

The tar like substance popped like yolk cooking on a griddle, and splashed the Driver and the carriage, the driver gave a scream, and then suddenly was flung high into the tree-line, as if the tar had lassoed and trebucheted him.

Palmer jumped over the broken remains of the shell-man, and grabbed onto the rail of the door, in front of him was Hayley, who reached out and grabbed his arm, covered as it was in ooze and tar, there was a sudden convulsion as the bite ran through her flesh and she bounced back as if shocked, crashing into the far door of the carriage.

Palmer ran to her, grabbed hold of her body, the pain in his hand was intense and throbbing now. Hayley was unconscious and her arm began to swell as the tiny pock-marks of the limpet bite dotted her arm like needle marks.

The sores spelt out a pattern that read like Braille upon the skin. Palmer did not know what it meant, but felt the language of the wound speaking to him.

"*Time is up.*" It said.

The lights in the carriage went out one-by-one.

The carriages were full of two or so dozen screaming, anxious, terrified people.

The darkness permeated the air, a thick soup of confused fear; the silence was foreboding and horrendous.

A single approaching light shone in the darkness ahead. Palmer could see the shadows it created on the track from the open door. He stepped out, calmly and quietly onto the dark track – aware of the eyes and the teeth glistening in the trees and the slither and trickle of ooze all around him.

He looked up the track and saw the light approaching, fast and angry. It looked like another train, the speed was awesome and breath-taking, but, there was no train.

It was ghost lights, and below it, teeth, chattering and chittering away.

Palmer closed his eyes.

Below him, even through his socks and shoes, he could feel the braille of the gravel speaking and pulsing through his skin.

"*Time is up.*" It said.

"*Time is up.*"

"*We feed now.*"

The light smashed into the train and carriages with such force and unrelenting anger that it was ripped to shreds as though made of paper.
Palmer held his hands up to guard himself instinctively, stupidly, as if such a gesture could help in the wave of a million nuclear explosions. The light seared onto his skin and he felt its expert sharpness cut perfect incisions to his core, every inch of his skin shredding and folding back to muscle and sinew and nerve and bone and marrow and then there was nothing more to cut too except the idea that was once a man called Palmer. The concept of the man, the psychic shadow of what was once a man.
The memory of Palmer was all that remained.

A wisp of an idea.

The last thought running through Palmers mind as the track, the tree-line and the train were obliterated in light and hunger was simple…

"I wish we had of driven to London now."

And then…
There was nothing.
Just darkness and silence and cold.
The feast over as soon as it had begun.

* * *

The Great Wolf.

For Garrett.

Every time Garrett opened the door he saw the shadow and he heard the growl, before the same padded, heavy-footed lumber could be heard on creaking floorboards approaching the door.
The rumble and terror of the glottal in the animals throat growing like an approaching motorbike.
Like a motorbike with froth dripping from the exhaust that was red with blood and had teeth the size of a candy bar.
A furry motorbike, with legs instead of wheels, and deep green eyes that had a distant awe and horror hiding within them instead of headlights. So a Motorbike that was a wolf - and indeed – not a motorbike at all...

Garrett was not very good at metaphors.

He shut the door with a sighed breath of fear.
He rested against it and cradled himself and rested his head back against the dark stained wood.

He could hear the creature beyond striding backwards and forward, and – for a moment – could hear it breathing, snorted breathes under the wooden doors half-inch wide gap between door and floorboards.
He span backwards and rested wearily against the wall opposite the door, reached up and flicked off the light in his hallway.

He was there alone now, in the dark, watching the shadow stood behind the door, the light between the floorboard and soft dark fabric draft excluder painting the shadow of the giant creature into the dark hallway, the shadow moving as the animal strode back and forth occasionally stopping to sniff the floor, snorting steam and smoke under the crack like some demented hell beast.

Garrett whimpered in anxious terror.
He shimmied and slid further down the corridor, holding his potato peeler out in a defensive prod before him.
What damage he thought he could do with this ridiculous weapon, he had no idea, but – it was all he was brave enough to yield against

the ghostly horror that stalked his corridor and was stopping him from getting out into the real world and – thus – kept him trapped inside this apartment day after day after day.
Left Garrett limply clinging to whatever fragile and tenuous threads of reality and sanity he had left.

Believe me…

They were fast running out and he was on an accelerated decline into severe mental health breakdown and a prolonged stay at shady acres.
Garrett understood this intimately, but what could he do to remedy the situation when the Great Wolf stopped him from leaving his home?

Potato peeler in hand, he made occasional forays into the hallway to see if there was any escape route yet available… and he smoked. Twenty or thirty cigarettes a day. Enough his lungs were black charcoal slabs that wheezed and moaned and gasped endlessly. Garrett liked the heavy breath and shrug of his chest when he was forced to take deep lumbering chugs of air to escape the noise of the animal behind the door.

He had tasted fresh air *once* and it had damn well made him heave into a bush; puce streams of vomit that cascaded from his mouth and nostrils and made him unable to smell for a few days.
He was happy with being an in-doors person – until recently – when cabin fever had suddenly and inexplicably set in.
Now, he was desperate to escape these four walls of his tiny apartment that imprisoned him, and he wanted nothing more than to see the blue skies and feel the arm draft of summer on his skin.

Often, when running away from the growl and stomp of the Great Wolf outside his door, Garrett would lock himself naked in the bathroom, hiding in the tub, under duvets he had dragged in from the bedroom, the bedroom which he was certain was being monitored by his boss at the insurance call centre, from which he was on an extended leave of absence due too personal reasons.

Garrett would hide under the duvet. The damp porcelain of the bath under his back soaking him and making him cold even as the blanket tried to keep him warm. He would hide here, and with a small battery powered torch, he would write journal entries explaining his quandary.

DAY 39:
The wolf is outside the door again today.
He sounds bigger than ever.
I woke this morning to his heavy breathing and the snorted venom of his lungs blowing under the crack, dust and disease blown high into the altitude of my flat, mixing with my oxygen. Polluting my breathing air…

He is trying to flush me out by making my atmosphere unbreathable.
I am onto him.
The four legged bastard.

I am going to try and escape this afternoon – I think I will have the best chance around tea time, when he gets hungry and realises he cannot break into the flat, he will inevitably go stalking for meat elsewhere…
This is when I will run to the elevators, take the express to the lobby, sprint to the revolving doors (everyone knows wolves cannot operate revolving doors) and then make good my escape by taxi to the grocers…
And there – I will feast like a king.

I am so bored of pasta and water.

And so the entries went.

39 days inside the apartment had sent him stir crazy.
But – really – Garrett was no better outside.
The people made him edgy and twitchy. The city made his skin feel like he had allergies. The traffic scared him in ways the Wolf could

never touch.
Garrett was a panophobic mess.
Yet, here he was, master of his own destiny, wanting to get out and breathe the unique city air again and feel granite and concrete under his toes, rather than splintered wood and dusty linoleum.

If only for that bastard Wolf.

He crawled out of the bath and gripped his potato peeler tight in his hand, edged nervously toward the door in the darkness of his apartments hallway. A short conduit between his lounge - which was a pizza box strewn war-zone full of full ashtrays, half drank cups of coffee *(in the middle of becoming ecological growth pens, cultivating several different strains of mould and fungus, some of which had names)* with journals scribbled on scraps and folds of paper, littered and thrown on every surface and his bathroom, from where he made his exit. In between was a small open gap, which lead to his kitchenette, a tiny box room with an oven and a fridge and little else, that smelled of damp and garbage.

As he walked down the hallway, he turned off each light, quietly. When he got to the door, the shard of light crept into the dark passage from the corridor beyond, under the crack by the floorboard.

There was silence.

No padding.

No snorting.

No breathing or low rumbled growl.

It was quiet and still.

Garrett put his potato peeler down and gently and as calmly as he could he put on his torn and soiled Converse, he reached over to the shoe rack and resting on top was a fur hooded anorak which he put both arms into, and shrugged it on, he reached for his beanie that was resting on a hook by the door.

He pulled up the hood and tentatively he reached out for the handle of the door, turned his key gently as calm and silently as he could. The *click-clack* of the door was amplified in his mind by a billion percent – and he felt sure that the entire complex could hear the mechanism turning and unbolt.

But – importantly – there was no reaction from outside.

The Great Wolf seemed to be conspicuous with his absence. This made Garrett nervous and eager in equal measure and with panicky, sweaty hands, he turned the brass handled doorknob, opened the door the faintest of cracks, the noise of the creaking and sighing door was like cannons going off in the middle of the night, like a million critics tutting at a bad movie.

Yet the Great Wolf was not there…

He allowed himself a smile, and poked his head out of the door gently and slow and looked up and down the corridor, scanning the hallway for traps or the telltale shadow and huff of the beast.

Nothing came.

Garrett removed the key and closed the door as softly as he could and stood flat against his door.

He began to shimmy against the wall edging toward the elevators. Once opposite, and still with no sign of the Great Wolf anywhere, he bounced from the wall with a push and took up a flat position on the wall opposite the two art deco elevator doors, his index finger angrily and incessantly pushing the CALL button.

The elevator made the BING noise that marked its arrival at each floor.

BING

BING

BING

BING

GROWL.

Garrett looked at the hallway left and right and could not see where the noise came from. He bounced off the wall and faced the two elevators, his potato peeler tight in his right hand, his keys – in case of emergency reversal of this plan – in his left.

The elevators carried on their journey.
BING
BING
BING
GROWL…

Garrett was sweating heavily now.
He looked down the corridor and could see his door, two hundred meters or so away and outside of the door was sat, massive and shaggy, dark furred and foamy mouthed, red eyed and with steam rising from it like some demented Baskerville hellhound that was on the verge of flame – the Great Wolf.

It looked at Garrett with hungry intent, Garrett looked right back – his eyes wide and terrified. How stupid he was to think he could escape and it to be so easy after 39 days of terror and harassment.

He fumbled for the potato peeler, unable to find it, he settled on raising his keys in a threatening stab motion. His brain and his body were arguing with each other in clumsy handed dread…
he fumbled in his pocket to find his peeler. His fingers were not working, and the way he was waving his keys was with loose threatening intention, but it was too late, the Wolf was already on the move.

Garrett froze to the spot and he could feel the first spot of warm urine on his khakis as he pissed himself with fear.
The Great Wolf was upon him and he reflexively threw both key and peeler at the beast and then wondered why on Earth he had done something so stupid.

Both things bounced off the leathery skin under the blood stained matted fur as though Garrett had thrown a ball of paper. There was no damage; no sign the monster had even registered the gesture.

As the Great Wolf was ready to pounce, his teeth bared and his glottal growl building to a violent crescendo in his throat, the BING sound went loudly in Garrett's left ear and the elevator door opened, he jumped in and the Great Wolf just missed his right shoulder in the leap. Garrett could feel the displacement of air as he fell in a fumbled jump toward the elevator portal.

Garrett smashed on the floor and threw out his hand onto console and pressed every button he could get his fingers on to get the elevator moving.

The doors slowly closed with a jarring stagger, Garrett huddled with his knees tights against his chest against the back wall below the mirror and he saw the Great Wolf turn and face him snarling as the doors closed.

He had escaped…

As the doors began to shut, and the Great Wolf was unable to make any move to get him Garrett allowed himself a victory gesture, raised a single middle finger to the Great Wolf as the doors finally closed and he triumphantly shouted:

"FUCK YOU."

The Great Wolf saw it.

He would remember it.

Garrett did not care.

The elevator was moving and he was on his way to the ground and daylight.

Finally free… finally safe… finally…

CA-CHUNK

The elevator shook, huge clunking noises and the sound of grinding gears and machinery. It gave a violent shake and then stopped moving.

The console lit up, every button illuminated and then suddenly, the whole box went quiet and dark as the electrics were cut. It shook one last angry time, and then stalled, motionless. The sound of creaking, groaning and the feint sound of tapping could be heard.

Garrett looked up at the roof of the elevator and a small red emergency light came on. He brought himself to standing, nervously and cautiously. Holding onto the rail around the mirrored walls tightly.

He opened the emergency phone panel.

All that was inside was a bare cable with exposed wires at the end. There was a piece of paper with scrawled black writing it read:

IOU 1 PHONE
HA HA

He screwed the paper up in his hand and threw it ineffectively against the mirror and slammed the panel shut. He looked up at the small LED camera and waved frantically, but, the light was not on. It was a dead feed.

He sat back down again and he put his head in his hands. Sighed and then nervously chuckled to himself.

"At least there was no Great Wolf in here." – he thought to himself.

"Small mercies." - He added.

Then the scratching came.

Every panel. Every surface. Every wall.
Chittering noises, and flapping.

A violent swell and shake of something flapping and beating the outside of the elevator - with it - a high pitched screech, the cawing of several hundred, possible a thousand or more, birds of prey. Garrett threw his arms out to steady himself, he crouched, and stared at the surfaces of the little prison he found himself in and he heard and felt the whole cube was surrounded by the birds of nightmares. Flapping and pecking and cawing and screeching and screaming for his bones and blood.

Garrett realised then that maybe - just maybe - there were worse things than wolves. He closed his eyes, pulled his hood over his head, and lay foetal, hoping that the sound would end, that the lights would come on and he could just live his life in normality again. It was a nice thought, but, he knew, deep down even as the birds pecked and clawed and dug their way through panels of thin metal that presented no barrier or problem to their razor sharp beaks and talons, even as he heard the first beaks chip and break through the faux wood panels and the mirrors surrounding him, even as the furious fluttering and cawing of Ravens and Crows and birds a dozen times bigger, that he was doomed.

This was his curtain call.

The Great Wolf was always followed by the Carrion birds. He knew that even though he had escaped the tooth, he would never escape the beak. As the birds burst through and flooded the elevator and dive-bombed the poor broken man inside.

Garret realised that with birds flying and swooping and taking hungry stabs at his eyes, he would never see normal ever, ever again.

***

Monologue / duologue.

Originally written as a monologue whilst at college.
I thought I could become the British Tarantino. Turn's out I couldn't

Please don't judge me harshly.

(The entry contains some themes that some readers may find triggering).

He collapsed into the bench, and he sat there, holding his stomach like a sprinter with a stitch. Eyes trying hard to find focus, and breath coming in bursts, a streak of sweat pouring from his forehead.
Nowhere to run, nowhere to hide, and his fate staring him down from the other side of the park.
This was how I found him; this was how he was when I eventually caught the bastard up.

So, you think you can run and get away…
Do what you did and get away from *me?*
Get away from what you fucking did?
Is that what you think???

He looks at me, pleading and begging, never saying anything, but his eyes never lied. His eyes stared through mine, boring into me and made it very clear.
He was guilty as a fucking sin.

Don't try talking you Cunt.
Don't try and get your sorry fucking carcass out of this.
I have the whole thing… the whole thing… all of it, from the girl.
She didn't have a single shred of the lies you have in your eyes, in hers.
She was an open fucking book mate.
So just keep it shut and listen.

He looks down at his feet, his eyes full of tears, of pain, of sorrow.
How he could possibly be sorry in this instant I do not fucking know.
How can he possibly feel sorry for himself for what he did?

I spoke to her.
I spoke to her for a *very* long time… she was singing like a fucking canary in the end.
Told me everything.
Sang like a bird she did.

I pause and I smile, and I cock my head like a little spaniel would, trying to catch his liars' eyes.
His dirty pisshole in the snow eyes.

Of course.
I had to cut her a bit.

Had to *bleed her* a bit.

She didn't like it. Screamed like a whore.
But…
well… after a few years of listening to those screams from slags like her, One, *well*, One gets used to it.

The screaming I mean.

And… I suppose, the cutting.

He looks at me then, pale, ashen face, like he had the truth at the tip of his tongue… a first for him, let me tell you…
but, as always - as they all do - he then sneers and looks away.

Don't you look away from me young man.
Don't you fucking think for a second that you can avert your eyes from what I have coming for you.
No one has done that yet, and no one will do that *ever.*
I have something for you – it's called *truth,* and when I give it – by god, you will fucking listen.

Just like your fucking whore of a daughter did.

I pause for effect, and he looks up, whiter than ever.
Still holding his side, still breathing like a fat lady in labour.
Pansy fucking Cunt.
Pansy little fucking waste of skin.

She bled like you wouldn't believe, *wooo weee*, she was a bleeder.
Hehe!
She bled like she was a stuck pig, if I'm honest.
Bled and bled and bled, yet, through it all she didn't lie once.
She never begged for mercy – which was good, because I have none to give - but the fact she didn't try, well, that meant something to me, it touched me.

If you take anything away with you from all this, take that.
Your daughter, bleeding, screaming, crying....

Not once did she lie.

Take that with you.
She was a good girl.

She really touched me.

So of course, I touched her right back.

He looks at me now. Those red bloodshot eyes nervous and sad, full of anguish, full of anger - muted, though it may be. It's there.
A slow ember burning behind his retina's.

I admit. I have to stifle a chuckle.

Oh god, did I touch her.
Deep and inside.
And she fucking loved it… She couldn't fucking get enough of it.

Bleeding and dying right there on your bed, she still got off on the touch of a real man.
The touch of a proper man…
Not the touch of some soft boy.

If, *y'know*, you get what I mean.

He looks right at me now bold as brass.
His eyes fixed on mine, and he stares at me.
A short frown appearing on his face, his complexion whiter than white now, his face pale, and deathly.
His eyes glazed, but focused.
Him staring at me, staring at me, not a quiver in his gaze.
He stares deep at me and he nods, chin resting finally on his podgy chest, tears welling in his eyes.
Staring at the floor, a stifled sob exploding from his mouth, and a bubble from his nose…
Messy bastard.

I fucking did her.
I cut her, and sliced her, and I violated her, like no one could imagine, and I did it, because… mate…
I could.

Simple as that.
I did her because I could, and because… *mate*… I knew it would kill you.

It would kill you a lot easier and a lot quicker than my knife to your gut could.
Look at you.
Holding your side, trying with all your might to keep your insides inside, when all they want is to leave your sack of a body and lay lazily all over that floor.

HA! Look at you bleeding like a stuck fucking animal.

See stabbing you when you weren't looking was just for me. I found it to be quite a fun thing. Simply a little fun thing for me to enjoy, a *bonus* you could say.

Telling you what I did to that daughter of yours, telling you what I did to that posing little madam, that was me doing my job.
I just killed you through her.

I am not a man of convention. I do things a little differently, a little bit more arty, and a little bit more…*tasty.*
Shall we say?

He still has his chin on his chest.
Tears still welled in his eyes, but those eyes now, they are white and vacant, pinhole pupils, and big void colour framing them.
Dead.

Dead as a fucking doorknob, dead as a slice of meat.
Hand on his stomach, a wet, damp bloody stain starting to pour onto his white cotton Marks and Spencer's shirt….
Dead. Just like I was paid to make him.

Dead from and through his daughter.

His daughter… poor sliced piece of bacon, dead and bloody all over the bed I made up out of thin air, and sliced with a knife that didn't ever exist.
Dead because it assisted me in killing him.

Dead. In my words to him.
But not dead dead.

I check his pulse, there is nothing but cold skin to my touch.
Not a blip, not a shiver.
He's already turning cold, despite the sweat that covers him.

I rearrange his hands, so they are casually in his lap.
I do up his jacket, adjusting his shirt, pooled and painted in his blood, slowly pooling under the ruffled material.

He looks like a resting angel now, no one would even know what happened unless they gave the poor bastard a shake.

I take a seat next to him. Quietly look out at the park, absentmindedly shrug some dust off of his lapel, and adjust his tie gently.
I take the pocket square from his breast pocket, gently dab around his eyes, cleaning his tears, wipe his mouth where an errant strand of droll has formed.
Fold the square neatly and put it back where it came from.

A few seconds go past silently with the two of us just sat, in the afternoon sun, enjoying the world moving at its own leisurely pace around us.
I give him a friendly pat on the knee.

I take a moment. And turn toward him, my hand on his...

Never met your daughter Frank.
Never seen her.
Heard you had one.
Heard she was a bit of the good stuff.
But never even seen a picture.

Could be doing her thing, right now, shopping, watching TV, fucking some lucky cunt in Newmarket.
Could be tucked up safe in bed and sleeping through a lazy day off.
I really… *I really*… have not got a clue.

Never seen her, never met her, never fucking touched.

But…

and you should remember this you nasty little prick… if there is even a semblance of spirit in that sack of a body of yours, your daughter -

Are you listening…

Are you paying attention, Frank?

Your daughter just killed you.

The knife between your ribs may have done the damage, but the mere mention of her name got your poor old heart racing. Blood pumping through those veins and shooting round your arteries.

The mere mention of her, and your heart started pumping so fast that it just gushed that blood right out that neat little hole I carved in you.

So, yes, I did the cutting.
But your daughter, Frankie boy, she murdered you by simply existing.
You think about that whilst you rot in your little corner of hell.

Try and love her now.

I stifle another chuckle.
I take out the handkerchief from my coat pocket, wipe my hands, wipe my blade, fold it neatly and place it back in my pocket.

Slowly I stand, looking down on him.
Poor dead Frank.
Another job well done.

Bye Frank…
Sweet dreams.

Birds sing, the sun shines, and the clouds have parted and it's a lovely summer all over again. I give old Frank a polite salute. And turn heel to leave.

As I skip a two-step shuffle out of the park, back to my own private little paradise of a life.
Bye Frank…

Sweet fucking dreams.

***

Frequentcies.

Written for the TABLO online Flash Fiction competition.

*It didn't win.**
**I'm not bitter.*

Dancing Fingers...

Turning the dial like an expert safe cracker.
Fingers that moved so nimbly and beautiful over the knob, cranking millimetre by millimetre.
Backward and forward.
Gentle turns and touches.
Somewhere between the whisper and the silence existed the station frequency that had haunted them. The message clear.
The message life.

A pop of static again.
The teasing bubble of volume before radio silence.
The air was dead, nothing getting through tonight it seemed.

Above them clouds were dark, brooding, moody.
A smell upon the air of rain and lightning.
Jon knew that he had to find the transmission this evening, or the whole camp would start doubting his prowess as a Frequent.

He licked his fingers again, placed his hands upon the radio, as if divining for water. As if searching for a pulse.

His fingers danced balletically again upon the dial and the needle slid smooth and slow across the lines, there was empty air and silence, then bursts and crackles of gentle static then...

The voice.

Clear.

Clean.

Calm.

The voice at last.

"Jon" it said.
"Jon"

This was why he was chosen.
Frequents were one in a generation.
When the box called your name, you were holy.
You were God,
Every box they found spoke to him.

"Jon" it would say.

The gentle voice a woman pleading, begging, taunting, seducing him. From every box they found, on every point of the needle on every line of the dial; regardless of AM or FM, the voice was all that existed.
"Jon" it said.
"Yes, my love" he would say to it.
Never anything but his name returned.
"Jon..." and so it went.

Then today. *"Jon."* it said.
"Kill Jon." it whispered in sultry and persuasive tones.

"Kill Jon please."

And upon his lips were a thousand questions.
Frequently asked of him by the villagers.
"Why?"
"How?"
"Where?"

It did not matter.
The village had heard.
It was on every box, whispering at every bandwidth, every frequency, every station they had found.

"Kill Jon Please."

Frequents were like Gods.
They came once in a generation.
And just like Gods, they died savage and brutal at the hands of the sheep that once lay calmly at their feet.
The gentle bleats and bah's now vicious screams and baying roars.

"Kill Jon Please."

And the voice commanded, the village obeyed.
Frequent or not.
The Static whisper had demanded, so blood for blood and love for love.
No more questions.
No more whispers.

No more fingers dancing over dials.
The voice was gone.

And, so was Jon

***

3:47am conversations with God. Pt.1.5 (a *different perspective*).

A true(ish) story.

God woke me up last night, at three thirty in the morning, demanding that I speak to him because he was bored.
It wasn't all that much of a big deal, as not two nights previous, between the hours of 4am and 6am I had tea and pancakes with Lucifer in my kitchen, talking about the benefits of political assassinations in this current world climate.

No.
I was fine with God dropping by and visiting.
I just wish he would – *once in a while* – turn down the Host, as they have a terrible knack of jabbering at uncontrollable levels when you really want to just discuss plate tectonics and cloud formation with his imperial celestial majesty.

But. No.
Jabber, jabber, jabber… that's all they bloody do.
There. In the background, every time he opens his – *not insubstantial* - mouth, the whole of the Heavenly Host – "*Oohhing*" and "*Aahhing*" behind his every word.
And the big man sits there like he can't hear them.

"*Alright for him,*" I said, "*Being used to them and all, but me with my soft human squishy mind sometimes finds it hard to differentiate between voices, harp orchestras and the tingling sensation felt when God talks direct at you without aid of the Megatron.*"

"*Metatron.*" He said.
"*Whatever.*" I retorted.
"*You get the picture.*"
And, of course, he did.
He's GOD.
Capital *G.* Capital *OD.*

You see, the Devil is a good bloke to talk to about little things, the feelings of absolute hate you experience when the man in front of you in the queue to the tube farts and doesn't bat an eyelid as you are forced to walk through his fetid stench.

The feeling of rage that fills you when old people complain about how things are too expensive nowadays, with no care or visible knowledge of the idea and practices of inflation over time, and the pressure incurred upon the Pound by foreign monetary exchanges, yet – there they are, happy enough to sponge off regular tax payers and spend my hard earned money on food for their fucking terriers.
Satan, The Devil, Lucifer – call him what you will, he doesn't seem to mind.
He's a right belter of a bloke when it comes to chats regarding anger, emotional breakdowns and general lapses in humanity.

But God..?
Well, he's an absolutely different kettle of fish altogether.
Likes to chat about flowers, and fields, and animals.
Water flow dynamics, Temperature alignment and volcanic mass management.

He isn't a gloater, you understand, but he is very keen too big up his own work and, you know, if I had built everything we see in seven days, six if you don't count the half day at the end, Well, I would be a bit boasty as well.

It's just… sometimes, it's all a little bit him, him, him…
if you know what I mean.

So last night, when he suddenly changed tact, and brought this subject we hadn't spoken about before up, well, taken aback was I. Very taken aback.
You see.
There we were, me in bed and him on the edge at the end, never looking at me, for fear of burning out my retinas – of which, incidentally, he said:

"Making them, a piece of piss. Fixing them after they get buggered up? Well, even I am stumped. Sometimes, just sometimes me old mate, you kind of just

stumble into these things, and then you're stuck to leaving them to figure themselves out afterwards. Not worth the bother of playing around with the lovely little things, you'll only cause a mischief."

So there I am.
In bed, God at the end talking to me about what he has planned. Me, in my striped blue and white pyjamas, looking like a bad English stereotype, with the creator of all of the known and unknown universes sat telling me step by step what he has planned for us all.

"*You see - the thing is, and I don't mean this personally, but you are an accident.*"
He said.
"*Basically, there I was playing around with the stars and the planets and the celestial gasses, and what would you know – as these things happen, boredom sets in. There I am floating around, playing silly buggers with balls of ferocious, explosive gas, and chunks of ice-bitten frosty snowflakes, when I realise, 'There must be more to everything than this?'*"
He is still staring at my floor, nice enough to not kill my poor accidents of Eyes.

How lovely.

"*So I went off on a wander. It's amazing really, in the early days I was so busy doing everything single handedly before the Host that I was knocking stuff out with no thought or record keeping. Masse's of the stuff.*
But after a while it all gets so busy and so hectic I have no idea what's bloody what, and I decide 'That's that! I need a break' So I down tools, and stage a one man strike against myself. Pack a small bag and off I wander amongst the stars and portals of my universe"

I smile. As I often do when he talks.
More often than not because I have no idea of what he is talking about and do not want to appear rude.

He knows this. I know he knows this – what with him being omnipotent and omnipresent, but we carry on regardless, as he's polite like that.

"Thing is mate. I may be the creator of everything, and I may know all of everything in my creation, but – and here's the thing, it gets awful hectic at times in my head with the noises and voices and sounds of the omniverse cascading In and out of my noggin, that I more often than not just – well, you know…
Ignore them.
And so therein lays our problem.
"You see, Earth was one of the last things I worked on, lovely greens and blues - always been partial to greens and blues, but I left it too close to the oven…
Sun – whatever you call it. And, like a cup with a little tea in the bottom, left on a windowsill in sunlight, things start to take over and do their own thing.
Mold…
Humans…
The like."

Smile slowly starts fading.

"You humans were an accident, and you may have waltzed around like some free range chicken for a hundred thousand million millennia, but, in my frame of reference, I left you for thirty seconds, and look what you've done?
War, famine, billions dead, disease, hatred, religious persecution, suicide bombs?
The whole thing is a shambles.
And even though it will only take me a matter of an hour or so fixing the lot, that's not the point.
You've made a right mess, and no mistake.
So…
I'm ending it, and I am starting again.
I'm… to use an allusion you may understand better… cleaning the cup.
I'm bleaching the mug…
I am degreasing my soup bowl.

Bye Bye Mold… Bye Bye bacteria, hello shiny clean, blue and green ball of loveliness again.

He pauses.
Deep breath.
Huge wondrous "H*ope this smile makes you feel better*" grin.

"Oh… And I'm doing it tonight,"

God, eh?

What a cunt.

***

Kintsukoroi -

More beautiful for having been broken.

A confessional.

I don't know exactly when I realised that the anxiety attack was taking hold. I remember a cold clutching grip taking hold of my heart, and my lungs filling up as though I was submerged under water. I remember the flush of hot and cold from my toes to the top of my head, surging and flowing over me as though an electric current was being forced through my skin.

A sudden swell of panic, a moment of feeling like I was falling, and then - I was lost in the overwhelming rush of terror that the anxiety attack had forced upon me.
A second or two of free-fall before I was staring at the pavement hurrying toward me in slow motion, a deep breath as I braced for the impact that, strangely, never came.

Six months of these and I was still not ready.
Not prepared and none the wiser for why they were happening.
Today's attack was literally brought on by... well.
Nothing.
Sitting at my desk, one moment laughing with my colleagues and the next I catch Amber's eye as she smiles and looks over at me. The smiles drop, her eyes take on a shine of worry, she mouths -
"Are you alright?" and that's all it takes.
My eyes fill with tears, my heart is fit to bursting out of my chest, my stomach is doing loop the loops and my skin feels like its trying desperately to crawl off my body.

I shake my head, I stand up, and realise that my whole body is shivering and I am light on my feet, wobbling. I make it to the door, I stagger down the stairs, I card myself out of the building and into the world outside. The sun is blinding, by now my breathing is a gasped glottle wheezing and struggling in my throat. A fine sweat is covering my body and my eyes will not focus.

I don't know when they arrived but Amber and Dani, my colleagues, are in front of me and are asking if I am OK. All I can remember is how hot it is, despite it being early April. How warm and fresh the sun feels. How clean the air tastes. How much I don't

want to be here right now and wish I was anywhere else.
Their words are hazy, fuzzy, rest in my ears like treacle.

This will be my sixth attack in six months.
The first happened on a Friday morning because I did not prepare my clothes for work the night before. A sudden case of option paralysis made me have a near total shut down. I couldn't breathe, I couldn't think, I could not stop crying.

I threw on whatever was still rolled up and nearest my shaking hands at the end of the bed, and I dragged myself to my car and sat with my hands white-knuckled on the steering wheel, tears streaming down my face, my heart fit to pounding out of my chest. Unable to properly breathe, unable to properly think. A soup in my mind and thick behind my eyes.
No idea what was happening, no idea what to do to control or stop it, and a deep sense that I was drowning on fresh air.

Mental health is strange like that I suppose.
The idea that you can live your life for 39 years and never have a single second of problem with your mind or body, and then, because you didn't get out your clothes for the next day you can literally be sat in your car and feel like you are about to die.

Each attack since then has been unique in its own despicable way. Each new attack brings with it a new series of emotions and feels more like a ridiculous roller-coaster held together with string and sellotape.
Standing at the door of a plane, at thirty thousand feet, with no parachute - and jumping out, hoping for the best.
That is my mental health.
That is my panic attacks.

The only good that comes from any of it is the introspection and self-reflection that you are kind of forced to engage in. Healing from inside out and finding meaning in each meaningless episode.

Soon, you start to find parts of yourself that needs that extra attention. Parts that are damaged with micro-fissures and tiny fractures that soon will expand, crack and turn into vast gorges and canyons in which you will somersault, without ever thinking about it first.

You hold up the mirror and you recognise certain aspects of your own life or psyche that need adjustment. The choices that you have previously made and the consequences that form the reality that you then reside in until the next momentous cross-roads. Until fate opens up a new fleeting adventure with your own body and mind that needs to be conquered and beaten.

And, believe me, you will beat them.

It feels insurmountable to start with; it feels like you are Theseus against the Minotaur, David against Goliath. That you are storming the beaches of Normandy with a water pistol - but then, you realise, that these were all events that were won by virtue and the heroes in the end. That each challenge is not just one for your mental health, but to help make you evolve and grow and become whatever it is that you were supposed to be.

That this - THIS - is a growing experience despite how horrific it feels when it starts. How horrendous it feels when you are in the midst of the attack. How lost you seem in the maelstrom of the moment - you will soon find that those who wander are not always lost. Sometimes it is a necessary part of the journey in becoming the best version of you that there can be.

Right now, I do not feel myself.
Best version, worse version or otherwise.
I am lost, and I am scared, and I am watching as all the things I love are affected by the detuned radio that is constantly playing in my head on full volume. Every now and then a flicker of the dial brings crystal-clear clarity and the most beautiful and mellifluous music. But - soon - the static returns and you are left with the chaos and the darkness again.

I have come to understand that the dark is not indomitable. It can be beaten and that once it is, the colours and light take on a stark new quality that is ethereal and also startling.
You appreciate everything a little more - and you understand that like any puzzle, the hardest challenges usually bear the brightest and best rewards.

Yes. I do not feel my best.
I do not always feel like me. But I am feeling like I am - understanding myself a little better each time this happens, and I hope that despite the fear of the challenge I can come out the other side the man I always hoped I would be.

I just hope that I don't cause too much collateral damage along the way. bSplinters have a tendency to stay long after the rest of the damage is cleared.
And splinters have a way of getting in everything.

Right now I am keeping my eyes peeled for splinters, and hoping that these cracks that are covering my body and my mind will soon be filled with gold, and I will be even more beautiful for having been broken.

***

Crash.

A dream, transcribed.

The sound of the twin engines screaming was what shook us first. The quiet summer afternoon breeze - being all that was chattering in the street - save the occasional bark of the neighbourhood dogs, or chirrup of grasshoppers which had dominated the afternoon air before.
The wail was something primitive and unearthly.
A sudden shrill squawk piercing the solemn summer air with a violent interruption.

The sound, first.

Then the sudden wind, that tore damp earth from finely manicured lawn. Stripped the branches of weak limbed leaves and made every single paned window explode in a crescendo of glass and dust.

The sound of jet engines over the estate was hardly a new thing. With air bases surrounding it, based east, west and north of the county. With the housing development being directly under the flightpath of the US airbases take-off and landing coordinates, and with the smaller airfield secreted away down winding country lanes not ten miles away in Kingswood where the roaring engine tests were performed for Rolls Royce and Boeing and the like.

Never the less…

This was not a usual mid-afternoon eruption, so easily accepted as second nature by the estates fair inhabitants. A momentary annoyance that soon faded into the otherwise uneventful daytime din.
This was not a hiss and roar of a dumb, restless dragon.
The snore and snort in short five second long burps.
This was different.
This was… elemental.

A rising whoosh of anger and rage that fizzed from nothing, a high banshee call, that acted as herald for the sudden gush of metal and death to come hurtling through the low tops of adolescent trees, to burst through briar and bramble, to bounce through field and the horse chestnut orchard that fringed the main road, to cartwheel over the long, high arching road that ran from top to bottom of the housing estate - sitting primly in the heart of the county of Buckinghamshire.

The twin engines belonging to an F1-11, which screeched like a demon in a fit of rage through the thin line of trees that bordered the furthest field between the estate and the small village of Edgcott.

The jet cartwheeling and digging a dusty divot into the field, before it hit the nearest fence, churned a huge gouge in the long ditch that ran parallel to Springhill road and flung itself now into a fiery Catherine wheel as it smashed nose first again into the potholed road, swiping Colin Goodgroves Maestro into the front window of Pete Chapmans lounge.

One further spin, what remained of the jet's wing neatly sliced through poor Paul Newman, eldest of two from 15 Springhill Road.
So fast was the bisection, that he had no time to react or feel pain, instead, frozen in shock at the outrageous noise, his stunned expression now whipped away as his upper torso caught ragged on the wings fractured, ragged armour-plating and swished him up and threw bits of him through the bathroom window of no.16. A macabre rain of Paul splashing and pouring down on the big corner yard they had.

Paul's legs still stood where he once did - But poor Paul was no longer whole, instead he was no more than jelly on the wall, window and lawn of the lovely Carpenters from no.16.

A small fire had broken out in the front living room of the Chapmans, and the Greens were now out of no.11 with their shotguns armed and ready for action.

The Cameron's of no.12 were in the kitchen. Where I began this tale. Where I was when the plane came down and hurtled into the old Cross household at no.23 Springhill Road. The remaining jet-fuel igniting in the final ten yards where it flipped on the side of Wayne Evans Ford Escort, and spun the car, the jet and the following debris - ablaze - through the porch, into the hallway between the lounge and kitchen and halfway through the dining room.

The cockpit struck the boiler, stuck upon the wall in the corner of the kitchen, and with a sudden WOOF the whole lot - jet, house, Escort and all - whooshed into a fireball and the air was simultaneously sucked in from every room and just as quickly as it was spat back out heaving.

The houses within 1000ft all groaned, those 2000ft out shivered, the ones 3000ft trembled... but those within five hundred feet of No23 - they staggered - back and forth - like a drunk looking to grab a lamppost and clutching only air, their feet going out from under them and the air pushed from their lungs - as they lunged toward the ground. Falling, in slow motion toward the concrete and gravel.

The whole estate shook with the explosion. The smoke and debris and fire flashed out in a heaving mushroom cloud that smashed every other remaining window.

The wave sucked in and effortlessly pushed out everything that was not stuck down or secured. The wave gathered the debris and the whole horrendous lot was thrown away and smashed through what was left of the street like shrapnel from a flack shell.

The sound was fury incarnate - a portal to hell, allowing out the Morningstar's scream. No sooner had the pantomime played out, the squadron of massive bombers came low over the horizon - a streaming red plume of twisting tendril smoke, thick like chalk and smooth like cream, as red as the devils heart - raining down on the earth, coating everything in a foamy skin. Staining grey streets crimson and the trees and floral and fauna a burgundy that was almost black.

What once was foam soon became a sticky, vermillion syrup, the consistency of smooth golden honey. Coating everything, painting the town red.

Those not dead from the jet crash breathed in the dust and the smoke and the foam-honey - and it coated them wholly. Soaking skin and plugging ears and eyes, nostrils and mouths. The groggy survivors of the explosion choking as they frantically scratched the mucus from their faces. Tearing off skin, peeling flesh from bones, scratching through eyelids and corneas, clutching out eyeballs, and dying - each and everyone - in a ballet of pain and self immolation.

Red on red on red.

The streets a sudden charnel house.

Those who were already dead now opened their eyes, as the honey turned to a thin, oily skein - smooth on their skin and fast evaporating, to a dewy sprinkling, and finally, fizzing away off their skin like effervescent mist, soon, twisting into smoke that popped out and into nothingness.

A whisper of a memory.

The dead now quite alive.

The alive, now quite dead.

Those in the open at least. Goodness knows what was to come of those yet to be pulled out from the debris and devastation.

It was only then that the spluttering cough of Paul Newman could be heard from the far corner of the big, corner yard.

"Can somebody help me...?"

Across the road, his legs had started to aimlessly walk in circles, tripping on stones and bricks, over doorframe and timber. A geyser of blood squirting in every direction from an artery that was jutting from the base of the spine that pointed accusatorially toward the heavens.

What was left of Paul's upper body (*what was not, lest we forget, jam on the walls and windows and remaining lawn of no.16 Springhill Road*) was a brutally disfigured, nightmarish mess. His head was hung limp from a neck that was obliterated and now in a right angle atop the diagonally sliced remaining torso. One arm was a marionettes, twisted, broken and caught within the ropes. The rest of the waist and the chest a ripped, minced, shredded cowboys sleeve. Tasselled and shaking in the breeze.

"I have a horrible feeling that I'm not in good shape."

It was then the howling began. As every dog left alive upon the estate suddenly all at once, together, got their hearing back and began to howl in pain. A nerve shredding, heart smashing, fear inducing low howl, as though the Earth itself had become wolf.

The sudden howl of every dog alive, working and talking as one. Joined by the harpy like whine and maw of the cats, the bleeting of the goats that lived atop the high fields above the estate, and the desperate guttural honk of the cows and bull that leisurely chewed the abundant cud in the lower fields.

Every animal, save the birds, quite suddenly a choir of one voice. A noise that chilled these now returned dead to their cores. As the first screams rung out like the Church bells - a wave of horror stories choking around the estate, and above the sound of the many fires, not least the inferno at the heart of no.23.

The animals were also hungry.

And there was only one food that would satiate this need.

The red streets littered with the dead and the once living.

Dinner was served.

* * *

Two flows to every river.

A confessional.

My job makes me deeply unhappy.

Everyday a monotonous, deeply unenjoyable, hard slog of eight hours reading case files and submission documents for police forces and private clients regarding crimes of the highest order. The most depraved and effecting betrayals of the human spirit and soul.

I arrive, I throw myself into it in the vain hope that by investing heavily, the hours will fall off the clock and everyday time moves at a glacial pace toward 5pm where I can finally turn off my overactive brain and collapse into the silence that is the car ride home.

This is my ritual, day after day, Monday through Friday. Only broken by those happy days when the sun is shining and the air is clean. The days when the rain does not pour and drench the streets and roadways and bridges. Those moments when I can step out of the confines of the four walls to which I am imprisoned between 9am and 5pm and can breathe clean air, bask in bright warm sunlight and stomp the impatience and worry from my bones by taking the walk around the canal.

This ritual within the ritual is a rare treat, but when it presents itself it can make even the dreariest, saddest, most haunted days shine incandescently. A total distance of 1.2 miles, the stretch of canal that lays parallel to my workplace is a ribbon of lush green and fertile brown that is full of animal life, insects and a variety of graffiti.

Half way up the waterway there is a Lock that is perched atop a small hill higher than the water level of the rest of the canal and which acts as a step within an incline in the pathway. From a distance the sudden rise in the path plays tricks on the eye and adds an air of mystery to the landscape.
It is here that I take my rest.

On these perfect days taking a seat on the thick wooden stanchion that acts as the arm of the Lock - that pushes gates closed and traps water levels to allow canal barges to traverse these arteries that spiral and flow from the River Avon - I sit, cross-legged on the oak beam, with music flowing like the Canal flows, the river flows, the ocean flows, within my ears.

I close my eyes and I meditate. Thinking of all the things that make me happy... or... not thinking at all.
Barely breathing.
Barely there in any real sense of the word.
I exist.

The energies of that canal flow through my veins like ethereal dust. Igniting and inspiring, no longer a creature of flesh and blood. In these solitary, solemn moments I am nothing but an entity of story and daydream.

Sixty solemn minutes is all I have.
Ten to walk to the canal entrance, ten to get to the lock, thirty minutes to allow my brain to turn off and take leave and my body to melt into nature's vibration and soak up the silence and stillness of the water and a final ten minutes to get back to work, having finally trudged the last section of the canal, rounding the bridge and back up to my office.

Back to the burden of proof and evidence, the never-ending phone calls and the miserable reality of the world. Yet, for a moment, a quiet lonely beautiful moment - the world is mine to bend as I wish with meditative pause and the flicker of inventive fire that ignites the second I close my eyes.

Lost, yet found, flowing freely like a carp upon the current.
Let loose upon the surge, free and innocent within the water.

* * *

Black and gold.

A future-shock fiction based on real events.

The black banners unfurled down the avenue on every pillar and pole. Long and sleek, material fluttering in the wind with a gentle flap and shiver. The gold indicia that was embroidered on it weighted the center somewhat, the sound of it dinging off the poles rang chorus like up and down the thoroughfare.

Shadows were cast, dark and foreboding on the pavement and road, so as to strobe inside cars that came and went from the tall dark towering building that stood sentinel in this bleak street.
The city was far from still, but today was eerily quiet.

The call and bleat of sirens rang out as had become customary since the final days of the riots. Pockets of resistance still existed in the city, but were few and far between now.
Purges had taken place almost immediately after the election, dozens of people rounded up and placed in internment camps that had been built in small suburban areas on the cities outskirts.
Surrounded by fields and lakes, away from prying eyes.

Overlooking golf courses, which still welcomed the country's mega-rich and privileged and sometimes saw the leader make unexpected and smug appearances; his permanent smile a smug slither of indifference and arrogance, painted stoic and fixed to his leathery face.

Oh God, *that face.*

Emblazoned on every wall and billboard in the city and across the whole country, the face stared out with slogans and tag-lines that were designed to nanny you into subservience, whose only intention was to drive home the lack of freedom and choice you had anymore in this burned out post-election landscape.

Four years had meant millions of people paying a heavy toll. Prices were non-negotiable and terminal. The hungry became the starved, the starved became ghosts. The poor became the dust upon which new skyscrapers and new extensions to the empire were built.

Television became a parody of the satirical shows that ran up to the coming of the first election that started the big turn inside the sprawling divided country.

Red versus blue to the death.

Brothers and families torn asunder by the need for one extreme or another, no middle ground found, violence replacing democracy and debate. The whole political process now playing out like some shady gladiatorial throwback, dividing lines drawn in sand soon bred into new borders in a country that was no longer a superpower but a waning flash of its former power on reflection.

The country turning out en masse in record numbers to cast a vote for the lesser of two evils or the greater of two lies.
The United States of America marching streets with their slipknots ready and prepared. Ropes upon which to hang itself on one of two bad decisions.

The Madman or the Legacy Candidate.

The Egotist or the Grand Self Publicist.

Either way, the country had buckled and braced the dogs, in readiness for them to drag the country away bloodied and broken and dying.

Only…
When the candidate was announced, and the primaries and the votes over, and the president elect announced, the country paused, breathed and stood silent and waiting for his next move.
And the Grand Self Publicist made good on his promise.
To make America great again.

Borders closed. Muslims, Mexicans and immigrants were deported in droves and numbers, staunch regulations at airports and

border crossings meant the country became an isolationist, isolated entity.
Diplomacy shrivelled up like grapes on the vine, relationships soured and age old friendships became complex and complicated enmities, all due to one mans twisted vision.

Yet.

America thrived despite the cold.

Agriculture bloomed, homegrown engineers and sciences meant that the farming world was reborn with a fresh vigour and impetus. People returned to work where they had been struggling for years on low incomes and lack of opportunities, welcomed into construction, commerce and industry. Farms were full of Americans subcontracted to landlords and landowners, living in cheap staff quarters and waking up mere feet away from their job, spending morning, noon and night entrenched in the building of the new backbone of The Leader's America.

The new techniques and industrialisation machinery that was borne from this period sold for massive profits to foreign consortium's, and money flushed straight back into the country.
The economy boomed.

For a while.

Soon, though, cracks appeared. Foreign policy had been all but wiped out. China stood at the gates demanding answers to why diplomats were ejected and why their businesses were being heavily taxed and fined for irregularities when America companies were being given relief and tax cuts. Canada to the north was soon looked at with as suspicious an eye as Mexico was to the south. Citizens were ejected for silly and beguiling reasons, moved from high and lofty positions to allow for American interests and assets to fill positions and spaces.

Soon, a new cold war was being fought at all fronts with Canada and China, whilst Mexico - being slowly but surely starved in trade embargoes. Paradoxically, whilst the familiar relations with friends were caught in this impregnable cold-snap, relationships with Russia were stronger than they had been in years until the second Cuban crisis, when the Cuban's economy started to boom due to the thawing of diplomatic quarantine — they started to become a new force in industry and medicine and when they started to accept foreign entities into their country to set up business and design new infrastructure on the old worn remains of the small Latino country, America viewed any and all moves by its neighbours as moves against its sovereignty in the area, accusations of spying and the notorious "Keys" incident, where a government cruiser was sunk with the loss of over 48 men, woman and children — in a case of mistaken intention and identity — lead to Cuba officially declare America an enemy of the state again, and Russia was pulled into the mess, alongside Canada — who also had dignitaries on board from a trade exchange.

America stood on the brink of a North America war for the first time in almost 200 years.

In the Middle East affairs were messier. Isis and Daesh had swelled with The Leader's appointment. Seen as an opulent figurehead of all that was obscene about the western capitalist states, the people throwing themselves into the war of ideologies became a critical mass event. Soon, the whole region was destabilised by The Leader's horrendous grasp of foreign policy. His own cabinet could not say no to his demands, and a new ground assault pushed America into the region in swollen and drastic numbers — a new Vietnamese-style tragedy ensued.

When a tactical mobile dirty-bomb was unleashed at the border of Egypt and Jordan, killing 20 off duty American soldiers and dozens more civilians, and a concentrated assault by suicide bombers, one of which was carrying a further dirty-bomb executed his assault on a barracks in the Southern Iraq safe-zone of Basra, killing over 300 soldiers and civilians and injuring scores of others, The Leader decided enough was enough and a tactical bombing campaign was launched on the northern stronghold of Raqqa.

Tactical nukes were deployed to the region onto Turkish bases, and an accidental bombing of a southern Turkish town by a lost patrol suddenly meant America was welcoming new enemies to the table.

An uprising in Turkey lead to the bases being overrun, the soldiers being slaughtered en masse and American nuclear weapons being seized.

Suddenly, the whole world was on the brink of a disaster.

Yet... His followers ate every word he fed them greedily and with rousing enthusiasm. His support was huge, driven by rhetoric and hatred and mutual stupidity.

His army was bolstered by his support of militias guarding his cities and towns and the constitution became a loose set of rules he frequently ignored. Soon, democracy was a looser term. America began to fall into his hands piece by piece by piece.

States who did not fall into line were denied tax breaks or much needed federal and government support. All and any dissent was met with penalties in senate, the screws on federal budgets and treasuries slowly turned down to a trickle before disappearing entirely. Scores of legislators were rounded up and overnight - with no warning, no words - were silently carted off to "Correctional Debriefs" - the new speak for prison. The two party system became a thing of the past, and all there was left was The Leader. Whose word was god.

The country had fallen into a fascist mindset with little to no resistance. What small resistance that made itself known were quickly swept away. Sympathisers and supporters soon removed from posts and positions and taken for correction. Few to be seen again.

Those who persisted did so from the safety of Mexico or Canada. Hidden outside of the borders of the great former United States.

Harmony no longer existed. All there was left was his word. Four years had seen the country shift into darker and darker shadows, and soon after the second election, which was muted and barely contested, delegates and candidates being besmirched and destroyed in press with smear campaigns and lies. The few brave souls who stood for freedom were ejected from power and position, and they too were arrested. Sent for correction, or killed where they stood.
Violence now America's second language.

The Democrats were driven into shadow and exile, and the country unfurled and stood lame and disunited, first under a red banner, then, under a black one.
A republic into a dictatorship in six short years.

Turkey still had the bombs.
When the American assault happened, three teams of Special Forces striking from air, land and sea to relinquish or disable the weapons, on that cold, dark Thursday evening in 2022, on July 21st, no one knew the danger that was about to be unleashed.

There were three bombs lost to the Turkish uprising. Three functional and legitimate warheads. Two remained in country, and were soon relinquished by the special forces, meeting strict and definite resistant forces. They took losses, but not before distilling the righteous justice that The Leader demanded. The third warhead had been dismantled and moved with no intel or knowledge of its whereabouts. It now sat on a boat that had left port in Caracas, having been shifted from European caucus to the Caribbean to the South American northern border in silent shuttling expeditions. Five boats and two planes, thousands of miles, if there was intelligence to advise where it was, the intelligence community was silent. The bomb passed like some token, silently and with stealth.

When the intel leaked from the mouth of tortured enemy fighters, it was already too late. Suspicions fell on Cuba, of course. Though they had nothing to do with it.

China now housed two garrisons of soldiers on the island, and the remaining channels of diplomatic power worked in busy, quick fire to calm down anger and distrust, opening borders to avoid all out war.

The bomb had already made port in Myrtle Beach, South Carolina. A former Republican stronghold, now home to enemies in its midst.

Democratic Freedom Party members…

like myself.

Hidden in plain view.

Fighting dirty in shadows to reclaim the country from the black and gold clutches of the Leadership and his twisted and mad grasp.

The bomb soon slithering its way in slow but dedicated fashion to the very gates of power.

Washington in its sights.

Redemption on its mind.

Freedom, a whisper, delicately poised upon its tongue.

Freedom.

No more black and gold.

* * *

The ladder tree.

A flash fiction written and submitted to the website HitRecord.
Based upon a photo by LinLouise

https://hitrecord.org/records/4487374

Each Ladder was a different colour.
Each colour burst in vivid vigour as the light that momentarily peeked from behind the clouds illuminated its rungs and rivets.
Each ladder led to a new and fantastic reality.
Once. And once only.

A tiny fissure in the liminal spaces between spaces, and the world you were a part of and the world beyond the final step merged into one, and you were gone in a blink of temporal wonder.
A breath caught heavy inside your chest. A million gallons of water heavily pushing down on your delicate ribcage, and the weight of the spaces between the spaces became as uncomfortable in a micro-second as the wet woollen clothing that clung and gripped you that time you fell in the lake.

Just as soon as you had held your breath and your foot had left the top rung, the ladder tumbled down and you were pulled up high and soon two realities - the one beyond the rungs, the one you were once anchored to like a boat in a harbour shaken and swayed by the early shivers of an approaching storm - and the one where possibilities were impossibly endless and ready to be delved into in open minded adventure, both blossomed beyond any comprehensible sense of colour and beauty and you were pulled hurtling through time and space to the new plain of possibility.

The ladder fell.
Plummeting toward the earth, only to be captured in the branches of the tree. Dozens of ladders now were locked within its branches.
It's muted mossy greens and browns now dotted with blues and reds and yellows and purples and greys of the ladders used and forgotten.

These keys.
These passports to the world beyond.

Each contained a tiny relic of the magic that they were once bursting with. Now, nothing more than strange baubles on the wooden skeleton below. Now, curious decorations within the lightning shaped appendages of the tree.
Each as strange and wonderful and out of place as you were.
They are hanging and suspended from the tree.
You, lost within these vast cosmic pathways, a small flat stone gliding and skimming the calm dark waters of the multiverse.

The ladder tree was a relic of all the times you had tried to change the world and yourself. And though you are *(or were, time travel is a confusing bedfellow)* never successful, you always find another ladder with the magic inside and you climb and you push yourself step after step, rung after rung to the very pinnacle of the ladder, and you touch the pinprick of light above you to open the gateway again, you push through to the other side.
Even as the ladder tumbles from under you, as you are pulled ever skyward.

The liminal spaces between the spaces, the breath between the breath, the light before the light. Another ladder, tumbling toward the safety of the branches below.

The ladder tree the singularity between you and the sky, the ground and the everything and everywhere in between.

* * *

260 billion to 1.

A piece of flash fiction written and submitted to the website HitRecord.

260 Billion to 1.

That's the statistic that dictates the chances of humans and humanity being the only sentient life forms in the Milky Way galaxy.

Just one galaxy in roughly 16 trillion brother and sister galaxies, the odds are crushingly against us being alone in this galaxy, let alone the universe.

Furthermore the odds state that maybe hundreds of thousands - millions maybe - of civilisations have been and gone way before we ever had a chance of finding them. Untold wonders rising and falling into galactic legend whilst we stumble around our own solar neighbourhood, like babies in the cosmic creche.

Yet - after countless years and resources innumerable - alone is exactly what we are. Every possible avenue exhausted - every planet and galaxy explored, physics and chemistry and biology re-written and rebuilt from first principle to last to cater for each brilliant new discovery that helped us on our search.

We step foot on the final unexplored planet and find that the barren dusty landmass is as empty, dead and lifeless as all 260 billion before.

Humanity, truly alone in the wide, vast and unending cosmos.

Screaming into the void, no answer in the wind.

* * *

3:47am conversations with God. Pt's. 2 through 4.

Confessions from the Holy Hotline.

2. BELIEVER?

Yes.
I believe in God.
In my line of work, you… you kind of have too.

I have, reverentially, and with no thought for my own safety or well being, prayed to his mighty heavenly majesty, three times a day, every day, since I was six.

Three times a day, like clockwork, rain or shine.

Once at 8.30am, before I leave my house to go to work…
Work?
What do I do?
Oh, do you know what? No one has asked me that before.
Quite exciting to be able to talk about it, if I am being honest.
Well…
I'm a Salvation Army Soldier of Fortune.

Yes.
The Salvation Army.

…I'll be honest. I have no idea why you are laughing.
I'm being *quite* serious.

If there is a job that needs doing by the SA, I will storm in, SA80 and Glock 9 in hand, Mylar/Kevlar compound combat knife on my belt, Strychnine and blowfish toxin in capsules in pocket… they are my favourite. Mix them in with a bit of bergamot, some tea leaves, sew the bag shut and flip on the kettle… they never see it coming.

I'll tell you. I work each and everyday with a gigantic smile all over my face, a giddy sense of bubbling excitement rising quietly in my chest, my insides all light and full of joy, and I will take out whatever problem or issue needs dealing with.

Political usually.

...Yes.
I suppose *you* could say that, I personally wouldn't...
I hate the term Assassin, it sounds so clunky, and obvious, so BLAH.

I prefer the term, "Problem Solver" or "Dedicated handyman" it has a much more working class shine to it.

Anyway.
The second time I pray is at 16.30pm, no matter where I am, what I am doing, if my watch chimes that little beep beep alarm that indicates it is 1630 hours, I stop and pray.

Driving, shooting, eating, killing... sorry, *problem solving.*
Regardless of what I am doing at that time,
It all takes a backseat to me having my two minutes alone with God.

Sorry?

Yes. Sometimes.

Sometimes that can be a bit of an issue, I wouldn't use your word – "*Inconvenience*",
As God is never an inconvenience.
It can be problematic, the act of praying, but it is never, NEVER, an inconvenience.
Of course, there have been some close calls. Some bullets that missed by a hair's breadth, some knives that cut, but just narrowly missed the vital organs and arteries... Of course... I know He is always with me, so I will trust in Him and I always make it through.

The others... Not so much.

Hah!

The third time I pray. Well, obviously, is when I go to bed.
And then, *then*, there is only one thing I pray for.

I pray that tomorrow is as much fun as today.

Yes.
You're right – absolutely right.
I do.
I absolutely love my job.

Now. Can I get you a cup of tea?

* * *

3. HIM.

It's been hard.
Very hard.
Honestly, at times – and I am not scared to say this to you, or have it recorded on tape.
At times I have struggled to find people to believe me and that really hurts.
It really is a very painful, hard, testing existence.
But… as is the way with these things.

You persevere.

See the first time, the first time, it was simple.
You walk from point A to point B spreading the word, and doing little things for the people, and they had no real choice but to believe you… because…

and I mean this sincerely… words – the meaning of them, the reputation, legend they created - it spread like butter back then.

It was a pretty meagre time to be around, the bloody Romans were everywhere, and finding a way to put one past the bastards was really what everyone was trying to achieve.
Then some bloke walks in, Jewish of birth, dressed like a right peasant but spouting words that seemed to be everything - everything you yourself were thinking - and when he says follow him, you drop tools and you bloody-well follow.

Reputation. See?
Legend…

At least, that's what happened at first.
Then things started getting messy, the old fella – he upped and changed his mind, thought some shock tactics were required.
And the next thing you know, there I am, stuck to a bloody two by four, in the baking heat, atop of Mount Canaan, and all I can think of is…

"Thanks a bloody bunch."

You know?
32 years old, nailed to a cross, and completely naked.
It doesn't, I'm sure you agree, get much worse.

But, there He is again, to prove me wrong…

Then some twat of a Roman stabs me in the bloody side with a giant spear.
"*Truly he is the Son of God!*" - thats what they had John Wayne say in that movie… What he actually said was..

"*Have some of that you Jewish Cunt*"
As he twisted the spear tip just that fraction deeper.

Ah, God.
My Old Man.
There He is again, to prove me wrong.

The second time was harder.
Much harder…

I came back in 1915.
I was born in St. Moritz, The son of a whore and a baker.
The product of a vicious rape in a kiln room.
Abandoned to the church, I was raised by paedophilic monks, some of which also had penchant for raping live animals and I was taught to read and write by a mentalist apocalypse worshipping friar named Peter.
He liked to whip himself with rose stems, thorns and all.
Lovely bloke.
Thanks Dad.

When the war started, I was happier than a Pig in shit to have an opportunity to get out of there.
I took up arms and joined his Kaiser's army, I was supposed to be the one to turn the tide of battle by dropping weapons and turning the fight into one with words, not guns and gas and bombs.

It was supposed to be simple…
Get in, spread his word, Get out.
With the old man on my side this time, apparently he was going to:
"Back me up to the hilt, none of that cross and nail bollocks,
straight forward word of God stuff."

Instead. I got in – got shot in the face within twenty minutes of hitting the frontline. It tore a hole the size of a fist through my cheek, obliterating eight of my teeth, smashing my mandible, and destroyed my ear on the way out.

I was taken to a field hospital minus the bottom part of my jaw, caught a horrible flesh eating virus from the less than sanitary conditions, and eventually died of a mix of dysentery and sepsis and was buried in a unmarked crate in the middle of a undocumented mass grave in bloody Normandy.

So…
Back to the drawing board we go.

And here I am now.
Living in a box, in the middle of sunny London, dribbling on myself every time I talk for all the teeth missing from my mouth - eight of them - because He likes the cynical irony of it all. Pissing myself daily to keep warm and eating decaying food out of vomit covered bins.

The people who do talk to me call me scum, the ones who don't usually spit at me as an afterthought and I have broken six ribs through constant beatings by other denizens of cardboard box city since I arrived. Not too mention the sheer amount of fellatio I have to take part in to earn money for a cuppa tea and a little rock of crack.

Yes. Crack.
When needs must my friend, needs fucking must.

I do sometimes catch myself though. Daydreaming, thinking of them up there, laughing at me. mocking me from a distance.
I can hear it all.
The big man, the winged pricks who surround him and coddle him, spurring him on, encouraging him.

And yes.
Sometimes, sometimes I do wonder.
Does he hate me?
Or does he just not know what he is doing?

Either way. He's made me look like a right twat and one or two more attempts at saving you bastards like this, and I will be honest, you can all fuck off, because I won't lift a finger.
Fuck the lot of you.

Some other idiot can give it a go.
Because truth be told.
Smelling like piss is starting to get a little boring.
And I'm not sure you arseholes are worth it.

What's that?
Oh.
Ho Ho Ho..

Fuck off.

No I will not sign your crucifix.

Prick.

* * *

4. DISSIDENT?

Don't believe in him, sorry.

That's not to say that I never believed in him… no no no.
I just don't believe in him *now*.
At this precise moment in time.

Once upon a time, way back, I was a devout follower of his.
But then one day, when I was nine *maybe* ten, my mum and dad took me for a meal to this lovely posh restaurant.

Candles on the table, fine violin concertos playing from overhead speakers, waiters speaking in faux French accents…
the bloody works mate.
I ask my dad, *salt of the earth fella* – would work a ninety hour week to provide me and my mum with anything we may need, anything we may want, right legend of a man he was – I ask him,
"*Can I have a steak?*"
And of course, being my dad, he says yes.

So we order a steak, me and him both.
And out comes this *huge* slab of meat.
Peppercorn sauce covered…
A perfectly cooked medium rare sirloin steak.

Size of a small horse it was, and tasted of heaven itself.

My dad, bless his soul, he takes one look at it and says:
"*God be braised!*"
And me, I laugh like a bloody idiot, because to me that particular play on words is clearly the best I have ever heard.
God level humour my dad had.
Not even Monty bloody Python could make that up…

Then my dad takes a bite – with a look like he has just had the best tasting thing ever to pass his lips.
He looks at me, and he raises his eyebrows in a cheeky little dance, smiling whilst chewing down on this incredible slice of life.
But before I know what is happening…
Something has changed.
His eyes become huge, his smile disappears instantly, his hands raise slowly from the knife and fork to his throat, fingers dancing in front of his mouth trying to sign out words that are not able to come from his lips.
A genuine look of satisfaction turning into a grimace of dishevelled blue murder right in front of me, the whole pantomime lasting seconds - but

feeling like days.

His face goes purple, he spits up gagging sounds, he clutches aggressively at his throat, he waves at anyone who will look and then, finally, he collapses face first into the gravy boat.

Dead as the dead can be.

And I knew it was because he made a joke at Gods expense.
And God, miserable old bastard that he is, doesn't get the joke.
And so, in a fit of miserly old bastard brutality he smites my old man down, dead.

The next day was when I started my one man mission to destroy God.
Nine or ten years old, and I decided I was to bring about the end of his reign.
All because He has no sense of humour.
That…
And he ruined steak for me forever.
Not been able to have it since, and not once been able to rinse the taste of that steak from that day out of my mouth.
No matter what I try to rinse it with.

Kills my dad over a joke and ruins sirloin for me forever.
I mean… It's just rude.
So yeah.
Don't believe in him, and don't care if saying that upsets him.
He'll be dead soon, and we'll see who will be laughing then, won't we?

Fuck him if he can't take a joke.

***

Those who wander.

A journal entry.

I used to be terrified of cities.

Big old things, gloomy, dark, smoke filled monsters that would gobble you up and spit you out.

Incomprehensible transport systems that were like nerve-centres of the beast and confused and perplexed in equal measure.

People all staring at the ground or dead-eyed directly ahead but always avoiding eye contact or any kind of connection to their fellow man.

Then...

I visited this little city called Edinburgh and just walked the streets until the lonely, wee hours, alone with music soundtracking my treks, and now, I have a newfound appreciation and love of cities.

London unfolded more of its secrets every time I visited. Birmingham became a labyrinth of new thrills and joy, even Leicester (*where I now live*) became a maze of beauty and beguiling discovery.

Every-time I visit Birmingham or London - even if it is to areas I have been a million times before - I discover wonderful new additions or strange, unique little shards of life in places I never knew existed.

Today my girlfriend is in a nine hour exam, one that could determine her future and the entire course of her next decade of life - and I am just walking around, no plan, nowhere I need to be, and I am just breathing in the life and the world around me and I am smiling, wide and toothy.

I live in England, and despite everything you read in the news or see on the TV or hear on the radio, this is a brilliant country we have. Some amazing places, some incredible sights and sounds and smells and sensations are conjured by the people and the architecture and the history and the glances of the future fast approaching.

I know things are a bit crazy right now, but whenever darkness starts to slip in, something amazing happens to drag us back to normality again, or, sometimes into a beautiful new dimension of supernormal, extraordinary brilliance.

I'm feeling positive - despite all the negativity and gloom that we are constantly spoon-fed at every turn, in media, print and television.

I hope that we find our potential and become as great as I think we can be... not just us Brits, but humans in general.

Until we know for sure what is coming I know I have these little forays into the world around and with the friends and family who I love and these random adventures that will always be there, and forever evolve around us.

Today...

It's going to be a brilliant day.

I promise.

There's a magic in the air and it wants you to know it has your back.

Let it in.

Just let that magic in.

* * *

Sunlit uplands, here we come.
A tragedy in three parts.

A trio of articles regarding an ongoing disaster.
Originally published on www.musicandriots.com.

(The statistics stated were correct at the time of writing).

Part The First:
Witnessing a car crash in slow motion.

1. What about Brexit?

An entirely partisan look at the United Kingdom's collective breakdown. The in's and Out's of one of the 21st Centuries first great follies.

My name is Andi James Chamberlain, and I am a Remainer.

Now, that sentence is enough for a fair number of people to end reading there and then. Such is the fervent chaotic partisan mood that has become core to the thorny clusterfuck of a subject that is Brexit.

You are either a staunch and critical Remainer, who opposes the whole ideal of taking a nine-iron to the head of our relationship with Europe and the EU, or, you are a fucking idiot...
Sorry!
Leaver... You are a leaver.
So tired and jaded by the idea of being a small cog in a greater machine. Angrily waiting for the time when we as a nation are able to clutch back "control" and "Sovereignty" and strike out again on our own in delightfully adventurous and prosperous ways. Once again retuning the island Britain into a GREAT entity on the world stage. Leading from the front, guardians of moral superiority and heroes to the greater world, as paramours of how first world countries are able to evolve.
Except...
Well. It's not really working out like that is it?

No. BREXIT is turning into something of an almighty iceberg crashing full pelt into the side of the Titanic in choppy, freezing Atlantic waters. Devoid of nearly any lifejackets and with leaky, woodworm ridden lifeboats.

What was promising to be a celebrated and historic victory has fast become a rotten, poisoned chalice that has corrupted the spirits and hearts of politicians, civil servants and dyed in the wool Leavers – and has turned a lot of ordinary, regular Brits who supported leaving the EU into braying, foam mouthed pseudo-racists, xenophobes and maniacs clutching at straws to find anything of what they thought they were voting for in the proposals put forth by the Prime Minister and her merry band of bastards.

Brexit has been one of the monumental catastrophes in human history. A farce that just keeps bringing in the big numbers – all singing, all dancing – a cavalcade of absolute misery, which doesn't look like its going to slow down or quit its stampede toward country wide suicide anytime soon.

* * *

2. The shitlist. Let's look at the villains.

Where do we begin when it comes to bullet-pointing the entire sordid affair?

The bus? - £350 million a week saved in tariffs to the EU we can give instead to the NHS? – disavowed as a lie within 24 hours of the result being announced.

The fact that one of the two main campaign parties in favour of the LEAVE broke just about every fundraising law there is, took assistance from Russian influencers and is run by a man (Aaron Banks) who seems to be incapable of not breaking financial laws – and has one of the smuggest shit-eating grins this side of – I don't know, Nigel fucking Farrage.

How about how the UK public who were in favour of the Leave campaign were spun lie upon lie upon lie to the point that were you to ask a man in the street now what they voted for and whether it is in the proposed deal we have on the rickety table that is the negotiating bureau Theresa May has been cry-wanking over since she got her massive razor sharp banshee talons in the poison chalice left to her by the coward David Cameron – he would have trouble not haemorrhaging from his eyes and spewing stomach bile on you there and then, right before he bursts into flames.

Am I bitter about the whole fucking affair?
You bet your left bollock I am.
Right now we are a country in the iron handed grasp of a party of villains, psychopaths and nineteenth century throwback misanthropes who seem to all have their hands crammed elbow deep into the cookie jar, yet not one of them realise the biscuits are gone, the blood circulation is cut off and they will soon embolism all over the Irish backstop before they can get even a nibble of a crumb.

Brexit has been nothing if not consistently awful since the former pig-fucker in chief David Cameron called the ridiculously terrible idea of a referendum that literally had no planning, no preparation and no blueprint – despite us being repeatedly told, with giddy glee – that there was a roadmap in place, plans waiting to be actioned and the whole thing was going to be fine whether the vote said remain or leave.
The prime lie.
The original sin.
The beginning of the whole shambles.

* * *

3. Choking down the cold hard facts with bitter, spoiled milk. I'm not a statistician, but I'll do the math until one comes along...

So let's look at the facts.

There is a total of total of **46.9 million** people in the UK who are able and eligible to vote. Of this number, the voter turnout for Brexit was reported to be **72.21%**, which means that the result of the referendum - **51.89%** to Leave and Remain having **48.11%** - to break this down further, of the 46.9 million people who were eligible to vote in this process – whether for leave or remain – only **33.8 million** people participated. That means approx. **13 million** people who live in the UK or its valid borders, which were of eligible status to vote and participate in this election, did not.

The will of the people suddenly does not look like it is really being paid attention too now when we consider that present figures suggest that if the referendum was run again it is predicted that voter turn-out would be somewhere closer to 80-85%. Dig deeper and you find out that this percentile would almost certainly be in the majority for Remain - considering what we know now, compared to what we knew then – it is not hard to believe this thinking is true.

These numbers are eye-opening and sickening in equal measure when you consider that the referendum was essentially supposed to be only a straw poll. An advisory. Something that would allow the UK to return to the negotiating table with the EU and begin the process of finding a new deal that would be beneficial to us as a nation as well as keep the relationship and membership to the union alive, if on a slightly fairer keel.

The entire vote has no legal basis that decreed that we HAD to trigger Article 51 that begins the process and timer on us leaving the union. There was nothing legally binding about the vote at all. It was entirely advisory; to give us a better standing in future talks…
But, as we all know, the party that started this abominable shit-show decided to rupture like the haemorrhoid-ridden rectum it is and people either ran away "DOO DOO DAH"ing to a golden handshake retirement (Cameron. The coward) or turned into such backstabbing bastards that they caused what is looking like irreparable damage to the Party that could linger for generations. (Boris Johnson, Michael Gove and the irredeemably awful Ebeneezer Scrooge caricature – Jacob Rees Mogg.)

Do you want to talk about how in two years we have had two Brexit secretaries, one of which attended four meetings and did a grand total of what is looking like FUCK ALL toward negotiating any kind of realistic deal or plan, and, who is now putting his face on every TV show as he is able too giving his "Expert opinion" on the entire affair.

How about how the second secretary, responsible for negotiating the terms of the separation between Europe and the UK signed his name to the deal that is now being touted as our greatest opportunity and deal – and resigned the very next day saying he could not support the plan.

Hold tight.

I will repeat that.

THE ALLEGED AUTHOR OF THE PLAN WE ARE TOUTING AS BEING OUR BEST OPTION TO LEAVE THE EUROPEAN UNION IS NOW SAYING HE CANNOT IN GOOD FAITH SUPPORT THE PAPER, AND QUIT HIS JOB.

And to reiterate –

HIS JOB WAS TO WRITE THE DEAL THAT APPARENTLY IS NOW UNSUPPORTABLE.

* *The author of this article heads to the bar, pours himself a large rum - no ice - and downs it in a single gulp. After a second or two of grimacing, he pours one more and empties it directly on the floor* *

For my homies in Brugge.

* *He throws the glass at the wall and exits.* *

* * *

4. The farce knows no bounds.

How about we talk about how Prime Minister May refused to disclose the solicitors general and legal council's advice on the legal ramifications of the deal.
A decision that saw the government – and Prime Minister May by extension – held in contempt of parliament, something that has never happened in the entire history of parliament – an institute that has existed since the signing of the Magna Carta in 1215a.d (in one form or another, initially being the royal council that oversaw King Johns court, and which gradually developed into the parliament system we now recognise)

It feels now would be a good time to put the kettle on and take a moment of repose to take a breath, regroup and calm down.
This sounds like an amazing plan on paper, but sadly, in reality is as far removed from possibility as it can be – as I cannot stop thinking about how monumentally ridiculous this entire thing is.

We have a short window of time to finalise the deal – either with negotiated divorce terms, an agreed monetary settlement, a proper plan to cater for the millions of people who will be affected by this sudden tonal shift in regulations, custom agreements and citizenship challenges. We have a limited time to settle the ship to avoid further choppy, horrific waters and steer us clear into a future that doesn't stymie the future generations of people who are losing out on freedom of movement, the biggest trading block in the world and the largest unified council of nations on Earth – all of which co-exist in a complex, highly regulated and legally protected catalogue of benefits that we have enjoyed since out membership was ratified and agreed.

Instead, what we will have is between ten and fifty years of economic uncertainty, an exponential rise in food-bank usage and need, limited and one-sided regulation on movement to and from European countries, an entire motorway being turned into a lorry park because of the new customs requirements and a government system that is healing from the fractures caused by the almighty fuck-up forced through by a collective of pompous, self-serving aristocratic arseholes.

***

5. That sound you hear is a half a nation headbutting a desk.

Everything I have written above may come across as hyperbolic doom-mongering, however, much the same as the USA seem intent on a collision course of country and ruin with their führer Trump leading the country into near oblivion with his orgasmic stupidity, Theresa May seems to be having a game of oneupmanship with the orange wotsit overlord in the "how fucking stupid can we be this week" game. Deciding rather than to shoot off the whole foot in one go, it would be grander and more beguiling for the press and public to decipher reason and legend as they shoot off one toe at a time.

The facts sadly speak for themselves.

A crooked, deceitful campaign that contributed toward the result. A cataclysmic series of lies displayed as truth that contributed toward voters decision making and casting votes,
A cabinet of selfish, self-serving bastards who used the process to get rich quick and benefit as much as possible whilst doing little to make it fair or worthwhile.
A leader who is so obsessed with completing the job to secure her legacy that she is blind to the genuine will of the people – whilst forcing her own narrative and repeating how everything she is doing is to preserve democracy and the will of the people in the original vote… Despite changing her own mind a dozen or more times, moving goalposts daily and refusing to actually display any kind of semblance of democratic behaviour.

A contempt of parliament charge and a criminal investigation into one half of the main leave campaigns processes and organisers that will likely see several people serving real, significant jail-time.

The entire process from day one to this very day has been fraught with lies, deceits and deceptions – and steered to the brink of collapse by people with little in the way of qualifications to handle such a huge, life changing and landscape altering decision and process – that the limitations and list of indiscretions and mistakes are being highlighted and added to daily.

I speak not from a place of ivory tower, high-horse or arrogance – no. I speak about this from a land of fear, worry and anxiety that people with no real significant experience or skill are leading the whole program and are slowly walking us as a nation off the cliff and into the sharp deadly rocks below.

Millions of people will disagree with my thoughts, feelings and personal take on the mess, and more power to them for expressing such a thing. But it doesn't change the fact that I am right on a number of levels and does not change the fact that – though we were given a platform in which to express our opinion of the matter – in the form of a referendum, the decision made was not mandated by a majority of the populace. Rather, by a narrow margin of a minority vote, that will directly change the course and standard of living of every child in the country and a few million more who have lived here from inside the EU itself.

What Brexit is and what it will eventually become are still a mystery to me. As well as being the cause of a near permanent state of paranoid anxiety. As a proud Brit, who holds our history amongst the most important in the world – we have decided to take a blowtorch to thousands of years of precedent and decided that this would be our most famous folly in a deep swelling ocean of them.

I am angry that my unborn children's futures have been limited and stripped of potential by people who have never been, have no interest in going to and have never stopped to look at what Europe does for us, and how we benefit from its partnership. Instead, with closed minds and sad hearts, gladly voted down the opportunity to ACTUALLY be able to negotiate, by forcing a process we never had to trigger.

I am sad that this is still rumbling on like a limp horse toward the knackers yard, and I am confused as to why we have sat around and taken it without kicking off a second civil war to preserve common sense and our own importance as a nation and a historical entity.

My name is Andi James Chamberlain, and I am a remainer.
A tired, jaded, sad, worried, exhausted fucking remainer.
Who just wants it all to end and for this nightmare to no longer invade my every waking hour.

Brexit?
Bin it, mate.

* * *

Part The Second: The Dark Ages.

It has now been 1074 days since the Great Britain decided to vote itself out of the EU with a referendum that was called to protect one party from losing ten or so seats to a fringe party. 1074 days since the Labour party started the long but steady decline in the absolute mess it is now in, 1074 days since the Tory party of the UK decided that cannibalism and self immolation was a better look than the "Strong and steady" government they perpetually promised in the General Election of 8th May 2015. 1074 days since the Great Britain decided it was happier to be Mediocre (soon advancing to ABSOLUTE SHITSHOW) Britain instead being the once great nation it had enjoyed being for several hundred years.

Welcome to the post referendum, pre-Brexit Britain.
Where politics has basically become an image of pigs bathing in their own shit, and a comedy suicide of a nation as it struggles to come to an agreement on what Brexit is, how Brexit will work and what a Post-Brexit Britain is ready to be.

Up is down, down is up, cats and dogs are living together and it's the end of times.
Or so it feels.

Fuck. I am exhausted.

The referendum was supposed to be a statement of overriding intent, and instead, became a marginal success for 17.4 million people. 16.6 million people voted to remain in the union, a turnout of **71.8%** of the eligible voting population.
Since then, the tide has turned so that an over-riding amount of people who have since turned eligible voting age have stated had the referendum took place yesterday they would have voted Remain, and a

massive amount of Vote Leave voters have died. (P*rimarily due to them being old as fuck, or, more likely bored to death with the never ending pantomime that has started in Westminster and has not stopped for nearly three years now.*)

Welcome to broken, bitter, belligerent Britain – a country that is slowly kicking its own arse across the news, papers and internet – trying to prove that as hard as America tries to be the most obnoxiously self aggrandising country in the world, Britain has several beers it would like you too hold.

We live a life where Brexit dominates 90% of our time EVERY DAY, and the idea of what the hell is actually going to happen changes daily – so much so that I am positive the writers of this last season of the ailing, saggy bellied TV programme called "BRITAIN" really need to be sacked for stretching the fabric of disbelief into awful, ugly, terrible shapes and insulting our intelligence as an audience.

We have now had THREE Brexit ministers, two of which were as useful as acid filled condoms, and the third is basically a patsy for Theresa "Crocodile tears" May – who couldn't find it in herself to shed a tear for the 70+ people who died in Grenfell Tower fire, but did wail like a woman drowning in cut onions during hay fever season when she had to quit her job as prime minister for being an absolutely useless sack of shit.

Apparently we were supposed to be sad for her because of how tears humanised her, but I still believe she is about to pull out a photo of Eddie Furlong and ask if you have seen this boy, before turning into liquid metal and fighting Arnold Schwarzenegger in a smelting factory. She's a fucking robot – and you won't convince me otherwise.

No matter how hard she cries.
(*I hope she rusts.*)

Theresa May is a very short distance away from leaving her post as Prime Minister after failing to get her Exit Strategy deal through parliament THREE TIMES. A fourth attempt being the straw that

broke this particular robot donkeys back and forced her out. The conservative party has been cannibalised from within by a fringe committee called the ERG (European Research group) - a *complete misnomer* - as none of the members give a single shit about Europe except to count the prospective hundreds of thousands, and in some cases, millions, that they will make once we as a country get out of the EU's coffers and their private equity funds can start cashing in and maturing.
There are now 14 people running for the position of Prime Minister (and leader of the Tory party) – each one ranges in the category of "Mild mannered moron" to "supreme evil Super villain" with "bumbling fuck nugget" being the median way to describe the candidates.

It's less a personality contest as much as a FIND-THE PERSONALITY contest (clue: *They don't have one.*)
Choosing between Dominic Raab, Boris Johnson, Michael Gove or Jeremy Hunt for Prime Minister is a bit like choosing your favourite cancer. Or whether you'd prefer to lose an eyeball or a hand – they are bad choices which have no happy ending, no matter how hard you spin it.

It's a cavalcade of corruption, xenophobic, posh old Etonian's who believe they all have some form of divine right to be leader and therefore can MAGIC a Brexit that won't break Britain's ankle like that mad bitch from MISERY for the next 30 years.

In perfectly succinct terms, WE BE FUCKED.

Welcome to Britain. 2019.

My previous article about the Brexit shambles exhausted me to the core of my very being. And since writing it the Brexit car crash has continued to flip over and over and over, kicking debris into the stands and taking out innocent parties who just came to watch the show. It's buckled our industry, businesses are having aneurysms daily about the uncertain future that the politicians are promising will be all rosey fields of golden wheat and wonder – and the country feels collectively on the cusp of a giant civil war.

The Right have come back in a big way, taking the lead from our American cousins, and we are staring into a barrel of a gun trying to figure out whether it's being held by someone else, or we have our own finger on the trigger.

I have never been so scared, anxious and angry as I am right now.

Great Britain has a political system in tatters and allowing the rise of the grey skinned slug Nigel Farrage to come out of his hole and stand as an genuine contender as future leader – not 18 months after Jeremy Corbyn almost caused a upset at the snap election called by May when she realised she was out of her depth.

The future looks bleak. People keep talking about a 30 year adjustment until we start to see benefits of our own sovereignty. Brexiteers are fighting with each other on national TV about who's version of Brexit is better and more deliverable – and remainers have been labeled as terrible losers who are trying to derail "democracy" by asking that the final decision be allowed back to the public – and continually told by the powers that be that "the will of the people" only works once and needs to be honoured – as the "will of these new people" is less valid and clearly biased because we're all "snowflakes" or moaning "libtards".

Our evolution into becoming the 51st state feels complete and soon we will raise the stars and stripes over Buckingham Palace and roll over to let Trump tickle our bellies as good, loyal subjects to the grand American empire.
Jesus.
It is fucking depressing.

The greatest issue that Brexit has kicked up is the countries slow – but steadfast – decline into Far Right demagoguery.
The rise of con-artist villains like Nigel Farrage (*a man who has never held pubic domestic office, has failed four times to become an MP and who has wholeheartedly thrown himself into the life of tweed wearing, fox killing, climate change denial and fuckingTrump worshipping*) and his collective of festooned idiot disciples has tipped the scales in the UK and more and more white supremacists, far-right devils and pseudo-political experts have emerged to stake claims in what is "best" for the public, to try and divine the so called "will of the people" and to deny the facts that stare them in the face.

Let's not make any bones. Brexit is a car crash. As bad ideas go it is number one with a bullet. The decision to make it was one polluted with "Protest votes", outright lies from the players of the Leave side (spearheaded by the villainous Aaron Banks who has since been prosecuted and maligned for his actions) and a contentious battering of our parliamentary procedures. Including the death of one MP to an assassins bullet, and the death of several careers due to the entirety of parliament having such varied and wildly different views on what Brexit is, should be, could be, and probably will be.

In my view, anything that will smash the kneecaps out from under the country in every single meaningful way for a near on 30 year period BEFORE it can start to see any measurable improvement or benefit is not worth its sacrifice or the pain that will be caused.

But what do I know, I am a remoaner, and fucking proud of it,

In conclusion.
England is on fire, Wales are laughing at us and waiting for the exit to be opened, Ireland could soon be a killing field again, Scotland may soon hold its second referendum to leave the Union and will definitely vote YES this time to leave… The United Kingdom is held together with string and sellotape and the GREAT has fallen off the sign outside

Britain and has now reserved itself to laying in the mud, forlorn and forgotten.

We are a nation at war with itself and there is no end in sight.

Brexit.

As bad ideas go, this is where they go to die.

I just hope the death is swift and as painless as it can be; yet I know the pain will linger and the end is going to shift forever.

As I said.
It's fucking depressing.
Here's to the 31st October and seeing how this all plays out.

See you again in five months, I suppose.

Andi James Chamberlain
Crying into his lunch - 5th June 2019

* * *

Part The Third: In conclusion.

It's strange sitting here and watching seconds fall off the clock as the march almighty toward the hallow sunlit uplands of Brexit fast approaches.

No longer wandering what it would feel like to be a lemming, hurtling toward the cliff edge in giddy joy at our own demise. Oblivious to the certain doom that lays below.
Here I am. Living it.

Watching an entire country isolate itself into obscurity and confusion and self immolation. All for a feel of that lovely blue passport for a holiday to a country we could have walked into without any problems in June last year, but now we have to pay to enter and also get a visa for! The inconvenience is delicious! I want more please sir!!

Less than one hour to go until the country I have grown up in my entire life - Great Britain - takes the long walk out of the gold and blue draped hallways of Brussels for what is looking - for a generation at least it would be fair to presume - the last time.

Soon to begin the slog of figuring out exactly what the fuck post-Brexit Great Britain is when it's out there on its own, standing on the brink of the nest that has been its comfort and home for the last 47 years.
Determined to prove their worth at last to an aged and dying generation above who vividly recall the glory of the empire and the land before the Union with our neighbours... you know, back when the world was a torched and torn up cesspit of a bunker, dug hollow into some godforsaken (quite literally) trench in southern France. Determined to prove their worth and pay penitence in faith and belief that our elders know better. The country, the blood and futures of the youth and their own sons and daughters offered in sacrifice of worship to the grey skinned, pallid fleshed oracles of the yesteryear... before the Europeans, before the oppressive, aggressive shadow of the gently wafting ring of gold stars on royal blue.

Brexit is here.
We got it done.

Hip hip hooray.

*(A solitary partypopper limply *pffts* an ejaculation of lifeless chewed-gum grey streamers upon the drab grey carpet - like the exhaustive orgasm of some ghostly octogenarian.)*

Twenty minutes to go and crowds gather in "celebration and commiseration" and sky news so wonderfully put it.
Baying opposites - the gammon faced pit-bull leavers playing vanguard to the effete, old Etonian suit wearing grand Brexiteers - who quaff sherry and sip tiny spoons of caviar and giggle gently in feminine-tones as they peer jocularly over their half moon glasses. Thick brylcreem pomade sticking greying-at-the-temples hairstyles to oily waxen scalps. Giggles amplifying as the pit-bulls explode in rage at the slightest hint of snow.

Facing them socialist lefties with jumped up desires for fairness, equality, brotherhood and a shared value system upon which rests the greatest union of democracies the world has ever assembled. Pompous, pie-in-the-sky bleeding heart libtards who dream - NAY! - EXPECT a fair share of the riches, the land, the laughter and ale... expecting always! Never lifting a finger to earn it, the scrounging bastard rats and cockroaches that they are. These worthless rapscallions and dreamers.

The battle for the soul of the country ready to begin. As sensational and as inevitable as the awfulness of the last season of Game of Thrones. The cameras of the press, now tools of one faction or another, taking the lead of their cousins on the other side of the Atlantic *(another story for another time, fair reader!)*
The news primed and ready to unleash the tide of blood that's brewing on every TV screen from Lands End to John O'Groats, in epic 4K 3D High Def surround sound... history little more than tabloid fish wrapper now.

Ten minutes to go.
Tick tock tick tock tick tock tick...

Five minutes to go.

The relentless taste of our own knuckles still tastes as good the first time we started to punch ourselves in the mush. You know, on the day David Cameron doo-doo-doo'ed his way back to number ten, the day he resigned and threw the rancid, steaming horse shit of a casserole that Brexit was into the street for the next sorry bastard to fix.
Two minutes to go.

Fireworks weakly explode prematurely outside from some garden of a house whose value is likely to plummet in the near future.
A future looking bleak and very uncertain.
Here it comes.
Here comes Brexit.
Fucking yippee.

* *Great Britain cocks back the trigger of the shotgun, and gently fellates the barrel, rests finger on trigger* *

"GUGGBUH EGREBADDY!"

pulls trigger

Yay.
We got Brexit done.

* * *

Experiments in the erotic - Pt I & II.

The result of a challenge I set myself to dip into a genre I had never played with before.

I.

The water at first sprayed out at a temperature just a few degrees above freezing. The kind of cold that you could see on the lake most mornings, as creeping mist cleared its way across to the small island in the middle of the brown hued waters.

The sensation on her skin was a pure one - a little short of ecstasy, but edging the line between shock and sudden elation. Goose pimples rose like braille on her golden tanned skin and the hairs spiked as if a current of electricity had been pushed through her.

The sudden convulsion of the body had lent a sharp, not unpleasant ache that drove to the core of her womanhood. A shiver rippled through her hips and she tensed her pubic region tenderly, only to unclench as the water turned warmer and the shimmer of heat ran rampant on her body.

A wave of pure unbridled sensuality that scared away the goose bumps and instead left a smooth, velveteen feeling. The great tidal wave cascading into the slight bump above her clitoris, the barely one centimetre sized spot that touches upon the hood, running down the button, through her lips and deep to the crease of the buttocks behind.

She shivered as the temperature turned from cold, sudden and penetrating - to the lush warm glow that made her skin dance. Her skin became like a raw nerve, every drip, trickle and spray of warm clean water sending a morse code of sensation through her and the pleasure-sensors in her mind read it out loud -

P L E A S U R E – E L A T I ON – S E N S U A L I T Y

Each part of each word ricocheted through her mind as if the radio operator was tapping the message on the most sensitive parts of her. Each pulse and burst of the message tingling up and into her, rooting from her crotch to her brain and rushing back down again in shivers and tickles.

The dance again, between body and brain.

Her hands naturally wound up dancing too, long fingers pirouetting on golden canvas, toward that oh-so sensitive and hungry spot. Where the fingertips soon did more than just a gentle jig, and instead found a dance partner in the warm, sticky wetness.

Deep inside her there was golden warmth that felt like alchemy. The sensation building and budding. Her fingers probing in and around the lips and inside again, her fingers wet now not from the shower, instead, from the rush of warmth inside her. It dripped down her fingers, running down her thighs, her legs coming together and seizing around her hand.

Her mouth a delicious O-shape that moaned and gasped. Each push of her finger inside, each touch of her finger on the button of her clitoris sending a wave of shivering convulsion the length and breadth of her body.

The complex crescendo of climax.

The morning ritual...

Where her mind could wander on memories of men and lovers; boys from her childhood, gentlemen who had smiled on trains and walkways... every one of them a dance partner for a moment or two, as her fingers went to work on the folds of her glistening, warm wet flesh.

The sighs rampant and breathy. Soon... a hush within the warmth, the sudden burst of ephemeral brilliance, a flash of white... and an intricate judder of incandescent confusion as the climax took hold.

Every morning she would do the same.
Her shower was her favourite past time.

There was love here, a silent, secret love for herself and her body.
A perfect union of mood and motion.

* * *

II.

The first time a woman took me in her mouth I was 19.
I remember laying there, still and nervous, cold beads of sweat bubbling to the surface of the nape of my neck.
My fingers grasping at the cloth of my bedsheets, thin cotton taut and stretched beneath my fingers.
A gasp of breath caught lingering on my lips, clinging lazily to the back of my tongue. Held by a string of saliva to the throat that was warm and engorged red with blood.

The pulse throbbing furiously in my neck.
I could hear it thudding.

CHUD DUN
DHU DUN
CHUD DUN
DHU DUN

The woman had stripped off slowly and my mouth was warm from her kissing me. My cock felt harder than it had ever been from the gentle but exciting touch of her soft, warm beautiful fingers. At first they slowly stroked and gently twisted on the shaft, soon, the pace was more determined, more frantic.
The first drops of excitement clear upon the tip, wet between her knuckles, as she held a fraction harder and smiled with a serpentine shimmer on her mouth, the tip of her tongue poking through her teeth, licking her rosy red ruby lips in lascivious hunger.

I remember watching as if the act was playing out in slow motion. Her hand upon my chest, strong sharp nails scratching gently down my skin, as she kissed across the plexus and down across my belly - pausing only to look up and smile with feline eyes a tempting, temptress grin. Her tongue whipped out and licked my hips, her lips plump against my thigh, and then... the act itself.

As her lips took me, her mouth hungry for my manhood, I remember feeling as if I was falling underwater. Drowning in a captured moment of ecstasy. A lingering death that felt as perfect and as sensational as mans first glimpse of daylight after months of darkness, the first bite of an apple after seven days fasting, or the first hungry gulp of air after the riptide pulls you under the wave.

The more she took me, the deeper I went, the warmer and hungrier her mouth upon me, the more my heart felt like it was too beat out of the cage that was my chest and rattle the bones from right out of my own frame of a body.
This was a small death - *un petit mort* - that was caught upon a second that lasted for an aeon.
The blood left my brain, my heart and my limbs and re-routed entirely to my cock... I felt as though I was a mighty oak caught within a tempest.

The warmth and wetness and the deep pull of her mouth, her fingers around my tight, taut, hard skinned shaft, the uncontrollable arch of my back as I thrust deeper into her throat and her muted giggle and sucker as she took me voraciously...
The seconds lasted hours even as I climaxed within her mouth. She taking every drop like a great thirst had compelled her.
Her hand drawing a line across her lips as she took care to not waste a single drop

Finally, I burst, gasping for air as the climax shook me to my very core and the tingle and the shake spawned through my every cell.

'Thank you' did not seem to be enough for what I had jus experienced, but it was all I could manage, weakly.

"Thank you."

I whispered it, my eyes still closed my heart still pounding.
Thick fingers gripping cold sheets.
"You're welcome, Doll." Came her reply, also whispered, her lips so close to my ear and the line of my neck, I shivered from the sensation.

I could smell the sweetness of my own self on her lips.
Combined with the scent of her, a gentle, aromatic perspiration.
She licked her lips, and I could hear the saliva and my come forming a string between each bud. The feint pop as she smiled and her lips parted.
"You're very welcome indeed" she said, as I felt her legs straddling my midriff, and her wetness pulled my cock inside her...
A new sensation taking over.
"Very welcome indeed..."
A gasp… a moan… a moment of misty-minded mystery as the clinch evolved, naturally, into something… more.
She smiled. Her hands on my wrists, my arms above my head.
Her hips pushed back fully and - our eyes deeply connected in a shared moment of bliss, I was all the way inside her, my lips breaking into a moan as…
Ah...
but, this, my friends, this turn in the tale is a story for another time.
The memory fades and I am alone, smiling, happy and content. A little shake of my head, this memory right now just for me and me alone.
Maybe I will share… maybe.

A story for another time.

***

Death comes to dinner.

A story about an end.

A "ONE MAN AND HIS DOGMA" Short story.

(Please Note: This story contains themes that may be triggering for some readers).

For as long as Daniel could remember, he had wanted to die.

He had lived for too long as a shadow living in corners, unknown and unloved by his fellow man. His shitty little job pouring over numbers of high-class businessmen who were worth more than Daniel six or seven times over. His string of failed romances, all of which ended with him being told – YET AGAIN – that, yes, it was him not them and - yes - size did matter. His broken-down car, sitting in a pool of its own automotive blood – rusting and falling apart one piece after another every day.

It was fair to say, Daniel had dreamt of death.
He had become something of an obsessive over it.
Books and books and books on the topic were at present bowing the wood of several shelves in his rickety old bookcase.
He had watched documentaries on survivors of near-death experiences, so as to garner some idea of what he could expect from the cold grip of deaths embrace.
Not to mention the times he had skirted around the borders of death itself with several near-misses - experimenting with overdoses, electric shocks and - on one memorable evening - a liaison with auto-erotic asphyxiation that resulted in terrified flatmates, wetting himself spectacularly in white briefs and a midnight visit to A&E.
The first of a few unexpected visits, the most recent of which was only a month and a half before thanks to a handful of sleeping pills and a few ecstasy tablets and a quarter bottle of vodka,

He had egregiously made excuses and pleaded, teary eyed and beside himself with faux anguish, with cousins and uncles, aunts and complete strangers to make sure he was present at seven of his nine distant families deathbeds on the moment they had shifted and passed from this mortal coil.
Sharing no personal connection - except for those he had invented to be there in the first place - with the person whose coil was imminently shuffling. He wanted for nothing, except to be present.

He just wanted to... watch.
To observe, taking mental notes of all the minutiae of the mise en scène. The anticipation, the barely concealed grief bubbling up from deep within the assembled throng, as they finally hiccupped and gasped their final breath.
Paying special attention to any shifts or shimmers within the moment that were unexplainable - any shivers in the atmosphere or air around the person, things that he had convinced himself would exist;
he searched eagerly for the proof that would justify his yearning obsession and explain the cold stone that laid heavy within his belly his entire life.

The other two relatives of the nine who had died, had to carry on without his presence because his car had had its own near death experience - once on an A-road whilst travelling at nearly sixty miles per hour in the rain aquaplaning onto a soft verge and stuttering to a standstill, and once on the centre lane of the M4 when his motor had decided to just seize and stop as he had come off a slip road.
Both times he was fine with missing the main show with his relatives, as his car was playing out its own little death masque of its own, and Daniel loved only one other thing and that was a distraction from the boredom of life.

Yes. Daniel wanted to die.
However, as these things usually pan out in the great pantomime of life, he simply could not. Not because he did not have it within himself to see through his dalliances with suicide - as horrendous and as inexcusable as they were - but because he did not want to die before having had a chance for one last (*and first*) important conversation with one specific individual.

Death himself.

So it was that he found himself where he did on this particular Thursday evening, in a drearier-than-it-should-have-been mid-May, just before dinner time.

There was perfectly set quaint late-fifties crockery spread out on the tablecloth - which stood garishly in stark contrast to the navy-blue painted walls of his apartment. The cloth a splodge patterned and nauseating blend of oranges, reds, browns and mustard tones. Heavy golden tassels fringing the whole rectangular table, dangling precariously from the cloth, hanging lower than it should. The chairs drawn close to the table were enveloped by the monstrous thing.

A variety of aromas spiralled out in calm steam clouds from the kitchenette of his cramped little apartment. Filling every room with a warm, homely feel.

The most delicate of the aromas came from the centre of the table itself with the expensive bottle of burgundy resting, airing, popped cork next to bottle, two pristine high decorative crystal glasses neatly laid out next to the plates.

Daniel opened the kitchen door, sauntered into the dining area, lit some candles and cheerfully tossed the spent matchstick into the bin. His flatmate Eric poked his head out from round the door, looked around, and smiled coyly.

"Danny boy! You got a hot date or something?"

Daniel gently smiled back, poured himself a trickle of wine and sipped casually.

"Definitely '*or something*' mate." He replied and poured himself a larger glass. "You are out this evening, right? I remember you saying something about meeting the lads."

His housemate nodded, entered the dining area and slowly, deliberately flattened out a crease on the corner of the tablecloth, tidying it up and making the cloth uniform to the table.

"I am indeed. Just headed back out. Me and some of the lads will be in the Clarendon later shooting some pool if you want to join us. You can bring your… erm… date." He smiled mischievously and gave Daniel the thumbs up. Daniel nodded and smiled - Eric took this as his cue to leave.

"I hope this all goes well Dan. Been a while since I even saw you in the same room as a girl, so I'm dead chuffed that you have come out your shell, after… well, *you know*, all that business before. Have a great evening mate."

All that business before was Dan being found in a puddle of his own vomit with an empty bottle of sleeping tablets by his snoring face. All that business was five days in hospital, being pumped full of God knows what and undergoing God knows how many hours of questions - before he convinced everyone he wasn't trying to kill himself, and instead, had just mixed his medication with too much alcohol and had had a bumpy evening.
It had been only a month and a half since then, but Dan had barely left his room. Of course, his housemate was not to know that the reason for this was all the plotting and planning for what this evening would culminate in. But for Dan, that was beside the point.

He waited for the click of the door latch, and Eric's exit. As soon as he heard the gentle CLACK of the deadbolt, he turned around and surveyed his dining area, checked the little details, straightened out placemats that were not at the correct angle, flattened out that stubborn corner of the tablecloth that seemed to just keep returning to a creased rumpled mess and then wafted his hand over the wine and sniffed heartily, enjoying the rich bouquet - he poured two glasses out in preparation. Finally, he dipped his head into the kitchen, opened the oven door - a mushroom and sausage casserole was cooking away nicely and the smell that steamed up the kitchen and turned the windows into murky mirrors was somewhat hypnotic in its heady mix of flavours and scents.

Dan poured himself a small glass of water, downed it quickly, poured himself another and then whispered gently to himself -
"*Right.*"

He reached into his pocket, taking three large pills out - after a second of staring at them, the room quiet and empty - he took them one by one slurping them down with a swig of the clear, cold tap water - counting to fifteen in clear, relaxed fashion between each pill.

No sooner had he swallowed the final of the three pills than the room went stiff and cold. The lights dimmed as though they were shrouded by a grey chiffon fabric, and there, stood in the doorway was a cloaked figure holding a walking cane ornately decorated and shaped like a scythe.

He was here.

Finally.

"Death, I presume?" Said Dan.

A huge grin was plastered all the way across his face.

The figure simply stood silently before him.

No movement, just a calm, serene stillness.

A bleach white skull with effervescent azure blue embers deep-set within the empty sockets of the eyes. Long skeletal fingers strongly grasped the handle of the cane that was pure silver and shaped like the blade of a scythe but wider, more polished and blunted. It resembled a golf club to the untrained eye, it made Dan smirk as he looked down toward it. If he was being honest, he had hoped - *nay!* - he had demanded to himself that he would see a full-sized scythe, if for no other reason than to figure out how the damned thing was ever useful or dextrous enough to be a reaping weapon for such a slight, bony wielder. Seeing that it was only a walking stick was a disappointment.

It immediately set his back up and made him angry that the legends were wrong, or that they had lied to him. He was upset that this figure before him was not as he had hoped.

The smirk was now tinged with a touch of sadness, yet, he stood fast and remembered all that he had to achieve if he got this evening right. He had a mission to conclude, and emotions were an unwelcome distraction right now. Emotions were for normal people, and Dan, he was anything but normal.

"I am he, that is named Death. Yes."

Dan nodded, curtly. He extended a hand and took a step forward toward the skeletal figure. Death, looked down at the hand outstretched toward him, back up at Dan, and the faintest look of amusement manifested on the toothy mouth. Ivory, contorting into a grimaced grin.

"Daniel Craig Hancock. Nice to make your acquaintance." Dan said, beaming, hand still outstretched.

Death regarded the hand again, and slowly held out his own confusedly. Long bony fingers cold and frozen, were you to touch them. Daniel took the bones in his warm flesh and briskly shook, his eyes and the blue sparks of Deaths not breaking contact at all.

"It is an absolute pleasure sir. I have waited a long time to meet you. Please, take a seat… I'll join in just a few moments."

Death - strangely - broke the eye contact first and also broke the grip of the handshake. There was something off here, but how "off" he could not yet tell.

"*You have been waiting? For me?*" Death puzzled, Dan nodded, that smile of his - all but plastered on his face, reflected widely back.

Clean teeth - white and myriad.

More shark than person.

"I've been a fan for a *very* long time." Upon the word 'very' Dan had tapped Death jovially, like an old pall, on his breast.

Death gazed at the person before him, pondered the impertinence of the gesture, the audacity of it baulked at him and had he had skin lining his ivory bones, gooseflesh would have shivered across it.

He gave a non-committed grunt - ever the poker player - and took a seat at the table. Daniel smiled wider still, and nodded as Death sat, slowly, a bony hand almost uncontrollably flattening out the persistent crease in the cloth.

"Oh, I am sorry about that. For some reason when I last washed this tablecloth that corner has just been a right pain in the arse. It never sits well, always curls up into a crease, regardless what you do to fix it."

Death looked down at the cloth, as it slowly creased back up as if on cue. "*A pain in… the arse… hmmm.*"
Death quietly repeated Dans word under his breath. almost as though we was trying the words on for size. Never had he said a sentence like it.
"Uh-huh. A pain in the arse." Dan confirmed, smiling still.
There was an unnerving nonchalance in his every gesture and action.
"Now if you will excuse me, I need to check the casserole. It would be an absolute embarrassment if I were to overcook it in such illustrious company." He opened the kitchen door, took a step inside, and then turned back cheerily and said -
"Back in a mo'!"

Dan retreated cheerily to the kitchen, leaving Death alone with a rising sense of confusion, at the dining table.

A silence froze the room, Death looked around, taking in the scene - the odd collection of books upon the pine dresser in the corner. The ugly little ceramic statuettes made by Dan at art school, dotted around between the books like strange reminders of some moment of fleeting artistic exuberance, memento mori of a time when Daniel had other things than Death pre-occupying his every thought.

Death was uninspired by the furnishings, but could not help but be drawn back again and again to the crease - no matter how much he tried to ignore it. His hand tried to flatten the crease out again, and again, and again… and again and again and again he was fascinated as the damned thing defied all attempts to fix it. Curling back up again into that awkward little crease.

Death tried once more - and was stunned when he looked down at his hand and instead of bone, saw a limb that was lined with sinew, feint strands of muscle and a slowly growing circulatory system of veins and arteries.

He raised the hand and regarded it - something akin to curiosity ran across his pallid features. Stone faced, blue eyes shimmering - before

quickly hiding it under the table when Daniel popped his head around the corner.
"Won't be a moment. I am sorry. Can I put some music on for you whilst you wait?"
Death had that strange sensation again. The shiver of cold across his bones. But now was unsure if it was the weird cheeriness of this man before him, or, something else entirely.
"*Music?*" He said. The word fell from his mouth like an echo across a giant hall.
"Music." Daniel repeated. The smile a permanent fixture upon that strange face of his.
"*Of course.*" Death said. Still not quite sure what Daniel meant.
"Oh, goody! I have an entire playlist… I think you'll love it."
He disappeared again into the kitchen, Death watched him leave, and was then suddenly surprised - a genuine shunt ran up his leg and he gave a little startle as the speakers that were in each corner of the room came to vivid, vibrant life.

"*All our times have come*
Here but now they're gone
Seasons don't fear the reaper…"

Death was confused. He was uncomfortable, he was perplexed. The music was not helping. He raised his hand again to look, and now, there was a thin translucent skein that stretched over the muscle and sinew. a gentle, almost imperceptible pulse gave a metronome beat underneath.

Death raised his other hand, and this was much like the other - chalky white skin, but still paper thin, and near transparent. He quizzically placed a thumb (*an actual thumb, fat and dextrous, no longer a stunted bone digit… by gad!*) over the thumping vein, and he pressed down - gently, curiously - so as to feel and listen to the blood coursing through the new alien veins.

Death didn't realise - so enchanted he was with the feeling of the beat beneath his fingers - but he had closed his eyes.
Eyelids over orbs.
Deep azure blue eyes were hidden under pale white lids - but a thin crack of luminous ethereal light crept out from the kiss of each lid - top and bottom - illuminating fine white and grey eyelashes.

When he finally snapped to reality again, understanding that his eyes were closed for the first time in his existence - a deep shudder ran through him - and he pushed back off the chair with a start and stood, gasping for breath.

His fingers reached up to his face - HIS FACE - Fine, delicate features and all - cheekbones, lips, a strong chin. Hands now palmed over every inch of the thing, and the chair gave up trying to be upright and collapsed to the floor with a bang.

"*Come on, baby (don't fear the reaper)*
Baby, take my hand (don't fear the reaper)
We'll be able to fly (don't fear the reaper)
Baby, I'm your man…"

The song played on.

Death was now staring into the garish golden framed mirror that adorned the wall next to the dresser and by the door, still touching his features, still gasping in shock and awe.
He looked back at the table, saw the wine and grabbed his glass sinking back the entire contents before pouring himself another with shaking hands. He flung that back too. He looked back toward the mirror and was dazzled by the beautiful, un-naturally pale face that stared back.
Picking up the chair, collapsing heavily into the seat, he sat back down, his head fell heavily into both hands as he desperately tried to understand what was happening.
Two things ran roughshod through his mind.
Where was Daniel and what had he done?

"Then the door was open and the wind appeared
The candles blew and then disappeared
The curtains flew and then he appeared
Saying don't be afraid..."

Without even thinking, The Reaper began to weep.

* * *

Daniel held on to the counter top to stop the shivering in his hands. His elbows were seizing up, his shoulders kept tensing up toward his ears and he couldn't stop his jaw from gurning and his teeth from grinding in manic painful circles. The pills were doing what he had hoped they would and he had a small window to enact the next stage of his plan.

With supreme effort he dug himself a tablespoon of salt, poured it into the pint glass of milk he had prepared, stirred it with gentle vigour and clutched it, with his other hand he held his nose as he threw the monstrous concoction down his throat.

A sensation came over him - like a full body contortion - as the white fluid slid down his gullet and hit his belly. It was a sensation of body and soul separating and for a brief otherworldly moment he was looking down on himself from on high. The kitchen ceiling was no longer there, instead, it was like he was peering down on himself like some spectator in the coliseum vivaciously watching the lions gnaw down on some errant christian.

There was a snapping sound echoing around this strange lofty vantage point and a delicate knock of wind chimes caught in a wafting breeze. Then a sudden feeling of elasticity - as though he was being pulled to an extraordinary length - muscle, sinew, bone all stretched out in doughy extremes, before he crashed back into his body, and was present again in the moment. The taste in his mouth was something really quite disgusting, but he reminded himself through the full body shiver which he could barely contain what the endgame was and he poured himself another glass and sunk it in one greedy, nauseating gulp. The shiver and full body contortion happened once more, Daniel settled in to experience the separation event all over again, before crashing back to reality in a jolt.

All part of the plan.

He held onto the counter top for another couple of seconds, gave his head a tiny shake, cobwebs removed. He popped his lips together with a smack, took a deep breath to regain equilibrium and pulled the casserole out of the oven.

In a fluid, balletic glide he wafted into the dining room with a huge smile and lay the casserole pot down in the centre of the table.

Death was sat with his head in his hands and looked to be gently sobbing. As the door creaked its welcome with Daniel's entrance, Death startled and stood upright stoically.

Daniel looked him deep in the azure blue eyes and his creepy disconcerting smile stretched even wider than before. Death realised at this moment that he hated Daniel. He hated him to the core.

"Well, I have to say, you look very… vibrant."

Daniel exclaimed, he walked close to Death and put both hands either side of his guests cheeks - regarding the features like a sculptor inspecting a great work in progress, Death stood frozen in a state of shock, horror and apoplexy. Who was this human to treat him… so… so casually?

"Beautiful." Daniel said gently, and flashed that shark smile once again. He gave a little giggle as he moved to his chair, beckoning for Death to sit. The entity in black before him stared back. Pale white cheeks streaked with tears and a bottom lip gently quivering with a combination of rage and exhausted confusion.

"*You should be dead already.*"

Death pulled a pocket watch from his robe, he unclasped the lid and regarded the face which caught the light with a twinkle shining a bright blade over his eyes.

The watch rhythmically tick-rocked away in his palm, a palm that was now fully developed, strong and milky white, clear manicured nails and fine silver flecked hairs on knuckle and wrist.
"*You should have been dead and done, and I should have been walking you over the veil the second I stepped foot across the threshold.*
How are you still walking… talking… breathing? It makes no sense!"

Death was now barely containing the anger that bubbled inside of him. A new sensation, this emotion. For an eternity he had existed far away and separate from such trivial human foibles as emotions and feelings. He was a grafter, a workman. Someone who was entirely enveloped within the confines of his job, and nothing else beside.
What was he now?
What was this delicate, uncomfortable flesh that ensconced his frame but a liability and a burden?

Daniel gave up trying to beckon the guest to sit and took a seat himself. He noticed that death had already helped himself to a glass or two of wine and smiled again, a turn in the corner of his mouth shifting the grin to smirk.
"Good wine isn't it?" he said, waving a hand toward the bottle.
"My parents favourite. For some reason, whenever a relative or loved one died they always got this exact bottle and made sure to gift it to the surviving family - whether they were sons or daughters, husbands or wives. This was their gift of condolence. I thought… given the circumstances… it was more than fitting."
Death was not impressed.
"*What are you?*" Is all he said.
Daniel took the bottle, poured the creature before him another glass and one for himself, and gave one final attempt to gesture for him to sit. When Death did not, the smile disappeared for the first time.
"Oh for gods sake you rude bastard, sit the fuck down."
Death did so without thinking, without wanting. His knees gave way, and he slumped into the chair without question.
"Interesting." Daniel whispered under his breath.
"In answer to your question, I am exactly who I said I was when you

appeared before me. I am Daniel Craig Hancock, nothing more, nothing less. I'm just a man… But one who has flirted with your side of things for as long as I can remember. Just a man, who happens to be a big fan of your work and who has wanted - for a very very long time - to sit down with you and share my admiration in person."

Daniel opened the casserole pot and the deep plume of steam and the rich heady aroma billowed out like a dragon escaping a trap, it swung and swept itself wildly around the room.
Death could not help himself but to close his eyes and inhale the amazing scent of the juices and gravy inside the bright red pot.
Fresh tears rolled down his cheek.
"Eat." Daniel said, calmly and quietly.
His eyes fixed on the guest in black.
Death opened his eyes, hesitated for all of a second, and then started to spoon himself the food helping himself too two huge sausages and a decent pouring of the gravy drenched vegetables. He dumped it inelegantly onto the plate before him.
"*I don't… understand…*" Death muttered, a crack catching in his throat. The pulse in his temple and in his carotid thumping away, each beat a thunderstorm in his head.
"You don't need too." Daniel replied. "So just eat."

Death complied. Shovelling the casserole into his open mouth, and chewing, swallowing and repeating, gravy rolling down his perfectly white chin, dripping onto the table cloth before him.
"Good lad." The smirk again. "Eat up, enjoy your wine, and I will tell you a little story." Death continued to scoff the food down, slurping back the wine. unable to help himself, hating even more how good the sensation was and how much better it became with each mouthful.
Daniel checked his watch, nodded to himself in some strange charade of an agreement - reached into his pocket and took out a pill, held it up out between finger and thumb, showing it to Death, and then sank it down with a decent glass of wine.
"I'm afraid today is not going to be your lucky day." he gave his head a little shake, rubbed his throat, and gave a stark little laugh.

"You see… I was dead. For a full thirty two seconds. Before my heart started again and I carried on cooking.
That thirty two seconds should have been it.
The amount of pills I have taken in the last few days, on top of what I have been taking for the last couple of weeks, on top of the near misses I had over the last few months… well… Anyone else would probably have been dead twenty or thirty times over at any one of the last one hundred days. Not me though, because… I had a plan. I had a mission."

Death paused his feasting, fork mere inches from his mouth, the drip of gravy onto his plate sounding like rolling thunder. Daniel rolled his finger to gesture that Death should carry on. The figure in black could not help but do so.

Daniel poured himself another glass of wine, he swirled the glass in little circles to shake the bouquet and held it under his nose. Closing his eyes he breathed in and soaked himself in the sweet, rich, floral wash of the scent. He then poured a glass for Death.
"Do this." And he repeated the gesture, swirling the glass, breathing in the aroma. Death tried to push back against the command, his hands shaking, but there was no control, there was no argument. His flesh was Daniels to command. He took the glass and followed his hosts lead. His eyes closed as he breathed in the aroma and it was as though a galaxy was suddenly born inside his skull, such was the potency and force of the sensation. A shiver rippled through his entire body, and he slumped back into the chair, his shoulders surrendering and his body limp in comfortable abandon. He closed his eyes, and his breathing became calm and resigned.
"*Is this what it is to live?*" Tears were rolling gently, in fat balls down his cheeks again. But he was not sad. These were tears of a confused, joyful kind. His hands gripped the arms of the chair firm but steady. His chest rose in heavy lifts and falls. Daniel watched him, like a lion watches the gazelle as it sips at the waterhole.
"Of a fashion." he said, and sipped his wine.
"I will be honest with you mate. It's never been to my liking. These emotions, these sensations of feeling and the burden of having to map

and navigate myself around their fleeting, butterfly-like attention span. Up and down - one minute happy, the next collapsing fully into the pit of despair. What makes you laugh one day makes you cry the next. Wanting companionship so badly you feel as though you will explode without it, then the incomprehensible suffocation of someone loving you. It's all… too much. It is… wearing."

He poured himself another glass of wine - went to drink it, then looked at his watch and first took out another pill from his pocket and put it on his tongue before washing it down with the wine.

"That's why I have been so busy with my experiment. In preparation for your visit. everything had to be meticulous. Down to the last minute. I'm a walking metronome right now and no mistake."

Death opened his eyes, a hand reached out for the wine glass, Daniel pre-empted him and was already topping the glass up to the brim.

"Please… Drink up."

Death raised the glass a fraction to offer cheers to Daniel. He gave the briefest flicker of a smile. Daniel nodded his thanks back.

"Let me ask you something…. if you would extend me the courtesy of allowing a personal question?"

Death nodded.

"*Ask away. Why not.*" There was resignation in his voice as well as his actions now. The thin lips stained red with each sip of the wine, his tongue was deep crimson as he allowed the flavour to roll over his palette and slip deliriously down his throat. There was a richness and deep, perplexing, beguiling layers to this new evolution he found himself spiralling within.

Daniel circled his glass between his finger and thumb and his other hand drummed an atonal beat on the table as he stared at Death with a singular intent.

"Have you ever wished to die?"

Death, put the glass down and pushed it away slowly, like a cardsharp pushing in his chips, all in on the gambit.

"I cannot remember a day where I were not entirely enveloped by my role in this universe. Not a singular moment where I am not the full living embodiment of the concept with which I share a name.

I pass through glowing gateways, through silky-smooth shimmering veils of thought; I walk the lands where others are unable to tread and I glide upon the whim of a thought to traverse myself into the places where I am called.

My existence is one of subservience and unquestioning loyalty to my purpose. My purpose is death - in all it's many guises and incarnations.
I am Death and Death is me."

Daniel slammed his hand down hard on the table. he pointed a solitary finger at the thing before him.
"NO." he slapped the table again, and his wine glass toppled and spilled, the red stain seeped into the material, the glass tapped against the corner of the plate before Daniel.
Death was amused by the sudden rash of petulance.
"*No?*"
"No."
"*What do you mean no?*"
Daniel held his own face in frustration. He rubbed his brow then threw his hands out toward Death in a gesture of anger and impatience.
"You didn't answer the question. You just spun annoying little riddles and boasts. It's the same shit as your cane. A cipher for the real thing, a parody of expectation."
Death smiled, he was enjoying the sudden shift in hierarchy. Daniels frustrations moving him down the order of master/servant.
"*Answer me a question, and I will answer yours.*"
Daniel froze, his eyes fixed on Deaths. Death gave a brief, chaotic grin.
"*Quid pro quo.*"
Daniel nodded. "Go right ahead Pale Rider."
Death took his wine glass, gently, deliberately sipped the ruby red liquid, and then placed the glass down quietly and fixed his gaze upon Daniel.
"*Why do you want to die?*"

Daniel did not hesitate in his response.

"I was five when I saw my first person die.
It was my grandfather. He had an inoperable tumour in his lung and practically the whole family watched him cough himself into a stupor everyday. Foam and blood building up inside of him, his chest barely raising as he struggled to breathe. I sat by his bedside for eighteen days, held his hand, listened to him when he could gather enough strength to talk - to share stories - and listened when his chest rattled like an old can of WD-40. I was there at his worst point, barely able to remember any of his best. The whole time, the only thing I looked for was a sign, a moment, when the pain would stop for him.
He was a good man, a decent man.
He raised my dad to be a good man, he raised my aunts and uncles to be good people - and he was a pillar of the community.
All I wanted was him to be comfortable, for him to have a single second of respite."

Daniel gave a little cough. A crack and shake in his throat. A slight tremble in his hands, that were clasped in prayer before him, resting on the table.
"My grandad didn't moan or complain though… not about his illness, not about his discomfort, not about the pain. He just tried to smile and would always be so grateful for our company and the love we all had for him."

Daniel picked his glass up and filled it with the wine. He slung the drink back, a dribble ran down his chin, and he absentmindedly wiped his mouth with his sleeve, leaving a plum coloured stain on the cuff of his shirt.
"That is… until one day… Just one time, I was alone with him and he had this panicked look on his face, his hand was holding mine and it just clenched harder and harder and beads of sweat ran down his forehead in cold, musky rivulets. He was frantically looking round and round the room - as though something was in there with us both. All of a sudden his hand went so cold, icy cold, and his face went from panicked and frantic to a sudden calm, determined look of understanding.

His grip softened - which was good, because he damn near crushed mine to dust in his own.
He looked down at me and he said…"
"…*He is here.*"

Death's eyes were closed, his head slightly bowed in reverence, he whispered the words in solemn clarity.
"Exactly that. You… remember?"
Daniel asked, a tear rolled down his cheek.
Just one.

"*Daniel… You need to understand, in my time on this Earth, ever since Cain brought the rock down on the back of Abels head, I remember all.*"
Death reached across the table, his hand, white alabaster skin warm to touch, held Daniel's hand and gave it a gentle squeeze.
"*I remember every, single, life. In turn, I remember every, single, death.*"
Daniel looked at him, and nodded his understanding.
"*So since your grandfather passed, you have wanted to die, so you could see the glimmer beyond the veil that calmed him and took away his pain, that made him like he was, for a second, for a fraction of a moment… before his final breath.*"
Daniel said nothing.
Death was satisfied with the silence. Daniel didn't need to speak.
Death gave Daniels hand a further squeeze in understanding.

"*I have walked souls of literal billions across the veil.*
Listened to the endless pleading, begging, demanding of allowing them just one more day, to allow them to live on.

The things I have been offered, promised and bequeathed in vain attempts at allaying the inevitable. The wealth I would own, the empires I would command had I only taken them up on their promises.
Not one of them, ever, turned my head.
All who I visited wandered on to the place beyond. Whatever that place may be."
Death smiled, it was a frustrated smile, one burdened by the toils of the evening.

"*I am not the one in charge.*
I do not call the shots, I am simply a humble, loyal, thankful employee to a higher purpose. Going about my duties with no questions, no demands and no desires.
Happy to just do my part."

He let go of Daniels hand, and relaxed back into his chair.
"*You ask me if I have ever wanted to die…?*
I answer no.
And my answer is true.
I told you - I am Death, and Death is me… I do not wish to die, but…"

Daniels eyes burst into colourful life, and he leant forward toward Death, giddy anticipation on his face, awaiting the Rider's words hungrily.

"But…?"

Death looked around, as though checking for ears and eyes upon him. Making sure that he and Daniel were alone.

"*But… my.*
How often I have wished to live."

At this confession Death gave a hearty sigh, his shoulders slumped as though unburdened by some hefty weight and he held his hands before him, as though relieved that all his cards were finally revealed.

"*That is my truth. That is my burden. I hope that this satisfies your question.*"

Daniel regarded Death for a quiet moment that felt eternal. He rubbed his cheeks and face and brushed his hands through his hair. He then pulled out a pill, placed it on the table, and with a single finger pushed it over to Death.
"I have a proposal for you, Rider. A proposition that I need to air, and you to tell me if it would be acceptable, possible and interesting to you."

Daniel scooped up some of the casserole and splashed it down in a messy splatter upon his plate. He took another, and eagerly tucked in, consuming a sausage with little resistance, raising his eyebrows at Death in a flirtatious fashion.

Death picked up his cutlery, and politely started eating as well.
With a swallow of a chunk of carrot, his lips licked clean, Death looked over at Daniel casually and nodded.
"*By all means, proposition away, sir.*"
Daniel took another mouthful, smirking, swallowed loudly.
Wiped his mouth with the napkin to his left and leaned back into his chair.

"I had a slew of ideas about what to do when you got here. I'll be honest, some of them were violent, some were noble, some were fantastical... Until we started speaking, I had no idea what I would do. It's important to know that."
Death nodded gently, he gestured a calm shrug of his shoulders - as if to say - "*I understand.*"
"But, I think I have been so fucked up, for so long, twisted up like a knot of rat's tails in my own head, that I didn't really have a plan - not a proper, well thought out, strategic plan - not once, at all."
Daniel absentmindedly pushed some of the food around his plate with his fork.
"I have been taking these pills" he tapped the pill on the table.
"For a few weeks now. A month and a bit. Had some close calls with them - never anything I was proud of, but, I had to experiment to get the measures right. Science shit - you understand?"
Death smiled weakly. But Daniel could see he got it.
"And I think I have cracked it - I mean, here you are, so at least I got something right, somewhere, hey?"
Death no longer smiled, but he agreed.
"*Somewhere along the way. Yes.*" A calm stillness in his voice.
"Well. I've also been taking these pills." Daniel pulled one out from his other pocket - it was a blue and white capsule, slightly larger than what you would expect from a pill of its kind.
"And these do the exact opposite of those ones.
Where those stop things and make things go soft and sleepy - these ones, they take a few seconds, but they eventually give your whole system - the insides and the giblets and what not - a proper little kick.

They wake you right up, but your nerves and muscles on edge, and get your heart absolutely racing."

He tapped the salt shaker that sat centre of the table with the blunt edge of his knife.

"Turns out, you take two of these…" he gestured toward the pill upon the table.

"Your heart will pretty much stop within two minutes and thirty seconds. If you take two of those, *with* two of these…"

he held up the blue and white capsule in his hand.

"With a couple of glasses of salted water - salted, not salt water. It's a strange distinction - but the adding of salt to standard water, turns out to be really important…."

Death smiled, and nodded. He understood a lot about the intricacies of death and its many, many causes.

"Then you will die… for a while. But before anyone can get to you, the magic is already happening inside you, and though your heart will stop, and you will be - for all intents and purposes - a goner, once those other two pills and the salted water get the message, its like a slow, build up of electric is gently pooling its energy in the background. Whilst your body is dead, and your mind is racing toward that bright white light…. this stuff is getting ready to give you a hell of a jolt."

Daniel smiled. He lay the blue and white capsule down next to the simple white pill. Death looked at them, and raised an eyebrow quizzically, intrigued by where his host was going with this.

"So dead. for thirty seconds or so - enough time for you to make your way over, but then a sudden jolt of adrenaline and my heart started again. And here I am. Alive and breathing.

Had I wanted to die, forever die, I could have and I think i'd already be gone on the journey toward whatever the hell you keep beyond the veil…"

Death gave a gentle laugh.

"*You are absolutely correct.*" He chuckled.

"But I needed to sit with you and have this moment so I could put to bed all the obsessive thoughts and feelings I have had since my gramps died. Since I saw that look in his eye and felt the cold terror and sudden warm happiness he experienced when you came for him...
In short, I needed to talk to you and see if you needed help.
Think of this as an audition, an interview of sorts...
I want to work for you."

Death silently nodded.

He took another mouthful of food, took his time to enjoy the flavours that flowed over his palette. He sipped back a slug of the red wine and wiped his mouth discreetly on the napkin next to his plate. He then regarded Daniel directly in the eye, a freezing, blue eyed gaze, Daniel did not dare stare away.
"*You have gone to a lot of trouble.*"
He gestured toward the table, the food, the wine, then he ran his hands up and down himself - no longer a thin, reedy skeletal figure - but a strong, corporeal being.
"*And you have given me a gift, this feeling of living, of life.*
From the blood running through these veins, to the muscle that is upon my bones,
to the food that now rests within my belly.
My first meal upon this world, and a fine one it is."
Death raised his glass, and Daniel returned the gesture.
"My thanks, my eternal thanks."
He slung the drink back in one gulp.

"*However...*"
Daniel put his glass down and looked back at Death, his smile fading.
"However?"
"*Time is short. And all your efforts are for nought.*
Time - you see, is something far more powerful than you or me.
I should know - for she is my sister.
Time and Death, two constants that know no end, nor any beginning.
Two concepts that have existed as long as the thought of existence.
My sister, you need to know, is not as amenable as I.
She has no such pleasantries as curiosity or desire, or need.

She is prosaic and wanton and thorough.

Without time there is no death, and without death, there is no time - entropy - you see, is the cosmic marriage of perfection.

Time and death. At the start we were there, at the end we will be there -

and as I have said to countless creatures when their time has come, the moment of your death is as set in stone and as unavoidable as the sun rising and falling and rising again.

You can no sooner manipulate the plan than you can pluck the stars from the sky."

Daniel had gone cold.

A bead of sweat bubbled on his forehead and slowly started to drip down his brow and temple. Soon, he was bleeding sweat from every pore.

"*You have really gone to a lot of effort and I honestly cannot thank you enough. It has been nice - to break bread with you, to quaff wine and to converse as we have. To try on this suit of flesh and sinew, and to be as human as I am able to be with you whilst we waited…*"

Daniel tried to pick up the pill that he had shown to Death but his hands were shaking.

He tried to talk but his mouth was numb.

His skin was prickly hot, and he shivered all over.

His eyes were panicked and mad now, confused and no longer in control.

"W…W… Waited?" He stuttered, his hand to his throat as he gasped for breath, his skin turning a wet shade of purple.

"For w…what?"

Death tried to smile, but the skin upon his bones had already started to fade and turn to a crisp, papyrus. The muscles and sinew had begun to wane and fade and - soon - what was left clung to the bones like a fine webbing.

No longer man, no longer corporeal.

Death was as he had appeared.

A reaper once again.

"For the inevitable."

Daniel tried to reach out in anger, but instead, only pushed himself away from the table and his chair toppled to the floor with a bang.

Death stepped toward his cane, looked at himself in the mirror upon the wall - adjusted his cloak and wiped a skeletal hand over his brow.

"Ah. As handsome as I have ever been."

Daniel clutched at his throat, then his chest and collapsed forward grasping the tablecloth pulling the entire contents to the floor with him in a cacophony of smashing plates, shattering glasses and the red wine bottle smashing into smithereens, the red contents making itself known everywhere in a furious red barrage.

Death spun the cane in his hands, round and round it went, and when he fancifully stopped its spin with a flourish and a loud THUD upon the floor it was a cane no more, rather, a long bladed scythe. Its ivory handle long and brittle but as strong as steel.

"A cipher no longer."

He held the scythe in the flat of his palm, balanced perfectly, out toward Daniel, who reached up to tentatively touch the blade, the edge as thin as paper left the smallest most perfect of cuts.

A ruby red drop of blood, dripped dismally down the blade.

Daniel had a moment of pinprick pain and then struggled a smile through his grimace.

Death tilted his head in a quizzical fashion, emotions on his skull-like face now impossible to imprint.

He knelt down toward the man on the floor. Daniel still chuffing and gasping for breath. Death pulled out his fine silver watch, popped the latch and then closed it with a muted *"AH!"*

"We are almost there. Don't worry. The pain will be momentary, the peace will last forever… though I feel it is only fair to tell you that your idea of forever and my idea of forever work on very different frequencies.

You see, after this…" he waved his cloaked hand around the room, over Daniels prone body, and then rested it on his lap.

"...I have a very important appointment to keep. And things will... change. Quite drastically I am afraid. But you were a curiosity. You were very special Daniel, I needed you to know that. Very special indeed."

Daniel grasped onto Death cloak, reaching for something to pull him down but no strength existed within him anymore.
Death took Daniels hand, sat cross legged on the floor, and whispered to the man comforting him as he choked.
"I want you to know that the first person I ever walked over the threshold to the land beyond was Abel. Dead at his brothers hand, an innocent life taken by the hubris of another man. Lost and lonely and confused.
At the end, that's all you ever are... you humans.
Lost and lonely and confused."
He clutched Daniels hand tighter.

Daniel was weeping now, his face a dark bruise colour, drooling foam around his lips, Death wiped it away gently, a simple act of courtesy that he had never allowed anyone before or would again.

"You will be the last man on Earth who dies.
You will be my last charge beyond the gates and veil, my charge to escort to the mists of whatever is beyond this place. My last ever... because... this world, this reality, is facing its own demise and I will go with it.
Time and Death. From the start of everything to the end of everything.
Finally - my time has come and another will soon take my mantle."

Daniel squeezed Deaths hand harder, a spark of optimistic hubris. Death softly shook his head.
".. Sadly, it will not be you."
He patted Daniel on the breastbone, a friendly, convivial gesture.
"Though, were there time enough and worlds - I would have been honoured to have extended you a day or two... to experience that which you desired so longingly.
That which you craved so desperately."

Death made his way to stand, and when he was at full height Daniels hand - outstretched and grasping for Deaths - fell to his side, his bright panicked eyes went muted and hollow.

As Death stood in sombre reverence at the final sigh of life there was a queer shimmer in the air beside him. A glowing, wispy, ethereal clone of Daniel.

The figure looked down at himself on the floor, food surrounding him, cracked casserole pot and broken glass and smashed wine bottle like a chaotic halo around his body. He looked to Death, and back at his body, and gave a weak smile.

"So… This is how it ends?" He shook his ghostly head.

"Barely a whimper and no sign of a bang."

He gazed sadly upon his remains. Death nodded sagely.

"*Inevitably.*"

***

With a surprising grace Death spun the scythe around his shoulder, behind his back and then bringing it down in a screaming swipe directly before him, he cut a swath within the air before Daniel.

The flap of reality was daunting at first, as there was an impenetrable void of existence beyond. A glaring hole of black unlike anything that Daniel had ever experienced. A black that gazed back at you as deeply and fiercely as you gazed toward it, and which permeated a hungry, lusty energy.

Daniel could not draw his gaze away.

Death pointed toward the void.

"*The veil is in flux because changes are already in motion.*

The never-ending cycle of change. The roaring, crashing ocean wave breaking upon the banks. Such perfect grains of sand, golden with the sun, blue ripples slowly reaching toward the highest point of the shoreline."

Daniel's eyes were stained with streaming lines of silver tears, his retinas bright white, and glowing a deep yellow warmth.

"*I can promise you only one thing…*" Death said, his hand outstretched and lovingly placed on Daniels shoulder.

"*That your forever will be just that - Forever.*

A forever that lasts as long as a sigh and as briefly as the slow half-life of a star.

You will know peace. You will know love. You will know happiness."

He leant forward to Daniels face, the two of them cheek to cheek as Death spoke calmly and with the hush reverence of a master imparting wisdom to his student.
"*And Daniel…*
your Grandfather is there.
Waiting.
And he is so excited to see you again."

Daniels eyes opened as wide as they could in a burst of shocked appreciation and love. His chest rose as though a thousand volts were forced through his veins. Every muscle tight with momentary rictus.
"*Go to him.*"
Death pushed the spectre of Daniel toward the tear.
The flap of cosmic fabric tore further, the blackness beyond spun unthinkable tendrils of obsidian toward the ghostly figure of Daniel, wrapping around his limbs, pulsing inside his mouth and nostrils and eye sockets and slowly pulling him in.
Soon, a pouring wave of white enveloped them both and with a "THWIP" sound the fabric sewed itself shut with a fizzing sizzle and both the blackness and Daniel were gone.

Death looked down at Daniels prone, vulnerable body. The container for the spirit, now as empty and as vacant as a can, rolling down a street caught teasingly by the breeze.

He looked around at the mess that had been created, at the detritus that had smashed around his body. It was a shame that the man would be left with this as his legacy, but, such was the way of the human race. Sometimes the mess we left behind in our final moments outweighs the value we added to the world whilst we were there and busily entwining ourselves around the lives of the people around us.

Death was happy that he had enjoyed the small diversion that he had promised himself he would take before the end of everything.
He was happy that he had charged every soul from point A to point B, from Abel to Daniel, to the world beyond.

No-one else now would know Death… not *this* Death.
Another would soon carry the scythe, wear the cloak and carry the pocket watch given to him by his sister, Time.
Another soon would take on the burden, and bring their own stamp to the role and the responsibility.

Death was happy that he had enjoyed an evening, at least, to live and experience the human condition. The taste of the casserole lingered in his mind. The fruity wine was fresh inside his mouth, even with his tongue now long shrivelled . The beauty of his body and face, heavy with muscle and flesh - made him happy to think about. Now, all he had to do was fulfil his final duty and close the loop on this version of the world.

With an absent minded gesture he ran his hand in a circle before him and with a simple flourish of his hand - drawing a line from his head to his belly, he opened up the universe again. With a final shimmer of light, he stepped forward and into the ether. Leaving the room empty and quiet, except for the slight drip of red wine from the upturned and smashed bottle and glasses, dripping onto the wooden floor.

* * *

Static shadows were painted upon the cold stone wall and there was a throb of intense discomfort permeating the room. The only light was from a half-dozen, oil-burning torches, lining the entire length of one wall.

The lonely, thin and weakly-framed figure of Death stood by a window looking out over a blank domain. Black was all that could be seen on the horizon less for one pinhole of light that stood at the northern most point of the sky. A slight, tender, blue-glowing aura circled it, a solitary star in the sky devoid of anything other than impenetrable darkness.

The light was a memory.
The lingering memory of the last man to die on Earth.

Deaths hands folded behind his back, the skin like a waxed paper stretched out over bamboo bones – so thin and so porcelain that he at first looked like a waxwork left in a position of repose in some museum of horror.

He flexed and closed his hand into a tight and taut fist, the sound was that of a wet clump of leather being wrung out of water. The click and grind of bones were that of birch sticks breaking under clumsy feet. The veins, blue, green and deep, dark purple became lengths of tough, gristly rope. A strength existed behind the intense weakness that was on the surface, deep below a strength of some significant and terrifying power dwelt and in the simple gesture of a hand being opened and closed it was evident that it was as honed and ready to be unleashed as a whip in a slave-trader's hand.

A door opened with a heavy effort, the static shadows lit up and shifted as if they were alive and trying to hide, for an instant the figures imprinted on the wall burst as if a flock of blackbirds at a gun report, and sought the sanctuary of anywhere that was not in the gaze of the man in red who entered.

Standing easily at seven feet tall if he was a foot, the man had a beard as big, busy and thick as a lion's mane, a deep strawberry-blonde, streaks of white bled from the corners of his mouth, down.
The beard followed the line of the man's chiseled jaw up into a messy burst of golden-red hair, the flame's light caught it and it too looked like it was bursting at the seams with terrific fury and flame-borne sentience.
"**My Lord, we have word.**"
His voice a boom of bass-heavy intemperance, an undulating feeling of immediacy, lacking any subtlety or patience. His voice was a one tone bark of indifference, you felt that if he had spoken to you a question it would sound like a command.

"*He is dead,*" Death replied but did not move. His pose remained calm and still, his voice a gentle crackle - distinguished and full of fertile authority. A regal timbre.
"*I know. Of course, I know.*"
The man in red went to reply as if to ask how, caught the words in his mouth, and swallowed them deep down.
Of course, he knew.
Of anyone in creation, it would be him who knew before anyone else.

"*Ready the Tribunal, tell them we are overdue a conversation. Tell them to assemble every councilman and woman, every single member of the board, there is much to discuss, and there are other things stirring. I see now that we are behind schedule.*"

The man in red clipped his heels and barked an affirmation. What he said would be understandable to maybe three people in the entire history of the universe we understand and can comprehend. Death, still stood by the window, impenetrably still, the perfect picture of calm was one of them.
The red man turned and held the door to close. It was easily three feet thick, oak-sandwiched between iron and gold, with thick, iron bolts and hinges and a handle that was fashioned like a horse' head; sinewy and angular, strong and proud.
As he was almost out of the room, Death turned calmly, hands still behind his back.
"*And War...*"
The red man stopped and fixed the pale man with an unsteady gaze, a solitary bead of sweat prickled on his forehead and was allowed to roll down past his eye, the fear of showing weakness preventing him from wiping it away.

Death had deep-set eyes that seemed to be almost perfectly black, but for when the light of the torches caught them, then they were the pale blue of the horizon when it meets the ocean, the intense crystal blue of ice, fixed in a face that looked like it would shatter should it dare carve a line of any emotion, not so much a skull, as much as a waxy, porcelain, china doll mask, young and beautiful, but affixed with a shiny, unsettling hue of the dead.

"**My Lord?**"

Death turned back toward the window, his gaze falling upon the pale blue dot that hung limply in the pitch blackness of the sky.

He slowly half turned his head toward War, stood statuesque and stoic at the huge door.

"*Ready the horses.*"

Death allowed himself and the man in red a sly, almost non-existent smile. The thin lips turning maybe a quarter of a millimetre in both corners upwards, a cruel joke of an inflection.

The red man caught the smile and returned it with a bright, toothy gape. He nodded curtly and exited, closing the door as if a giant bank vault. A gentle pop sounded as the lock snapped shut and once again the room was returned to its previous stillness. The shadows, one by one, crawled out of their hiding places and found their homes in static silence upon the wall again.

Lord Death raised one thin, slender and febrile arm with hand outstretched. A single finger and thumb reached for and grasped the light from the sky, holding it between his digits, its pale blue aura emanating a warmth and hum as it throbbed in his cold and waxen hands.

It had been a long time coming, but finally the moment was upon them, they were about to name their fourth, and the stories were about to become a reality. A million lifetimes of work was about to be brought to fruition, and the world was about to learn a new destiny.

The pale rider smiled deeply, as he gazed longingly at the weak blue dot between his finger and thumb, rolling it gently back and forth, before he closed his fist around it so hard his skin seemed to light up. Waxed paper skin became an amplifier for the light and life, as he closed the window with a gesture, and sat in front of a fire that burst alive in flame as if by magic in his presence.

As he paid regard to his hand, a pale blue glowing fist, he smiled slightly wider, a sick movement that shook the room with giddy revulsion.

Some things were not meant to smile.

Crocodiles and misery were but two.

This man was the third and the worst of them all.

His smile was a hammer to everything good about the world.

It was written somewhere that a vicious stroke of a butcher's knife across naked flesh would have made a better smile, it was a hard fact to argue, unless you knew for what he was smiling.

Death looked down at his hand, opened his palm, and said simply…

"…*Thank you, Daniel.*"

Before blowing the light away.

The light floated off his palm like a lone ember popping from a fire grate, flaking and fizzing and disappearing into dust and then nothingness. Death watched it as it faded into atoms. He watched the atoms pop and fizz and break down, and so on and so on. The entirety of the vast quantum universe kaleidoscoping away before him.

How did he fit into this madness of creation within creation within creation, destruction within destruction within destruction?

Was he just as chaotically breaking down into his component parts, each one another universe where he is sat before a fire remembering the unmemorable? Was that all that anything is?

An endless cycle of fizzing and popping until there is nothing left to fizz or pop any longer? Death tried to shake the thought from his mind, and instead chose to focus on the important fact that he would be forever the only thing alive that would remember to remember the last man who died on earth.

The memory of the man, of Daniel, sat pleasantly side by side with the faint, luscious memory of warm aromatic casserole and the taste of the rich, heady red wine.
Behind it all the echo of music played, pulsing away in his mind.
Quietly, obsessively.
His motivation now.
His engine.

"*Don't fear the reaper…*"
"*Don't fear the reaper…*"
"*Don't fear the reaper…*"

***

In Conclusion.

Final Essay.

Nostalgia… it can be a deadly, fickle thing.

The author William Faulkner said - "*Memory believes before knowing remembers*" and it struck a cord when I discovered it that this is exactly how HEAVYWEIGHT THOUGHTS came into being.

A lot of memories of things that I know I will never truly remember. Fragments of things, broken shards of stories and bent and bloodied verse - just waiting for a poem. And to dig into the piles of half discarded, barely constructed, semi-amateur forays into lyric writing, sonnet, long form poem and elementary verse has been a treasure in and of itself.

Playing at being an architect of some great archiving of early genius was mostly a fun affair. Sometimes it brought me to the edge of some personal battle of wits deciding whether a story was worthy of inclusion, or was just that fraction too embarrassing and amateur. Driving myself half-crazy trying to figure out if I wanted the fumbled writings of my youth to see the light of day, with all their fuzzy edges and rough corners.

It was fun, but it was stressful. And it it taught me a lot - the biggest discovery being that I was not some bard of extraordinary talent when I was younger, I was - more often than not - ridiculous, insincere and brooding in just the perfect amount of post teenage ennui.

It was a delirious experience to shuffle around in the dusty mothballed fuck-ups and turds I had secreted away from public view, and the odd peanut of brilliance I had forgotten entirely about. Some errant line of words that could unlock another, and another, and another - until you were chasing dominoes and scrambling together a new and better story.

So think of the book you just read as the middle aged archiving of the spare room. The misbegotten artefacts of a quarter of a centuries idle ramblings. A collection of things that came before - and a stepping stone toward that which is to come.

Think of it as a personal kick up the arse I needed to stop dwelling on the bits and pieces of yourself that have fallen off along the road to where you stand, and instead, get on with carving that niche of your own to make yourself happy. A nudge in my own ribs to remind me of how far I have come and how I need only look a little behind myself to find that key that might unlock the next big project.

I jump off here into a new adventure with novel number two. Which has - by now - been slow boiling for as long as the poems in this book have existed. The same age as the fragments that existed in my notepads and loose leaf paper folders, which ended up becoming the stories in this book.
It will be a big project - but I am undaunted now. I am kind of stoked that the history of my first novel/short story collection has mirrored the first poetry collection/second novel - with the two releases being smaller parts of a larger whole. It's cool how these things work out sometimes, these pleasing little synchronicities.

I hope that you have enjoyed the work in this collection, I am happy to call it a start. Poetry is still an evolving creature which I am trying to understand better. But I am so happy with what I have created here, and I am happier still that it is out there in the wild, free and untethered, no longer dormant broken pieces hiding in some dusty box, in some damp storage locker, waiting for a story to be a part of. I'm glad they have found a home, finally.

It makes me happy that they have a book to call their own.

It's been a year of self-discovery, of growing confidence, reinvention and creation. Writing for my own reasons, writing a little something everyday and seeing what sticks to the wall and what will end up in another notepad - to sit idly by for goodness knows how many years to come - until the time comes to drag out the archives again and do a volume two.

I'm proud of what has been achieved in this book - and - even when the stories are a little roughshod, even when I am second guessing myself reading them - wondering what the hell was going through my mind when they were originally written, even when I laugh out loud at my own attempts at finding my voice and style - I am glad that they are here, I am glad that they have a home, I am glad that you got to read them.
It feels like a circle has been closed, a chapter ended, and a weight lifted.

It feels good to unburden the treasure trove and move on with a clean slate, and a notes app full of new ideas to explore and time - finally - at my disposal to get stuck in.
Thank you so much for allowing me my moment of nostalgia.
I sincerely hope you found something - a morsel at least - on which to feast.

Until next time…

Andi James Chamberlain
Leicestershire, October 2021

About the author.

Andi James Chamberlain is the author of Urban Fantasy novel **ONE MAN AND HIS DOGMA** and short story collection **10 SHORT OF 31.**

He splits his time between Leicester and Stratford Upon Avon, UK - and When not writing works of fiction he is a music promoter, an abstract artist and a graphic designer.

You can support his writing work by becoming a patron at his Patreon page:

www.patreon.com/wordsfromandi

Or by visiting his official website:

www.andijameschamberlain.com

The end. (move along)